The Book of
Statistical
Process
Control

The Zontec Press
Cincinnati

ZONTEC

Published by
The Zontec Press
1389 Kemper Meadow Drive
Cincinnati, OH 45240
http://www.zontec-spc.com

The sponsoring editor for this book was Warren T. Ha; the editing supervisor and production manager was Richard K. Morris. Cover art production by Jean Green, Toledo, Ohio.

Many of the charts in this publication were created with Zontec's Synergy 2000™ statistical process control software.

Library of Congress Control Number: 2002105114

Printed in the USA
Fourth Printing

ISBN 0-9720994-0-9

9 780972 099400

We dedicate this book to our customers who have contributed to our success in the software industry and supported us across two decades of computer technology advancements.

Contents

The Book of Statistical Process Control

Foreword

It is only logical that a book to educate readers about the basics of statistical process control (SPC) should come from a company like Zontec, since the company's initial focus was on training and consulting—not software development. Over the years, we've observed that too many companies are looking for quick fixes and shortcuts to quality. Unfortunately, there is no such thing. Any company whose quality program hinges on this philosophy is surely doomed to failure. For without a thorough understanding of the basics, process improvement is virtually impossible.

On the other hand, workers do not have to be statisticians to take advantage of SPC. That is the reason for this book: to provide a practical, common-sense explanation of the underlying principles of statistical process control. The topics included in this book have been based on almost 20 years of exposure to the customer side of quality assurance. Readers should not find the techniques and calculations described in this publication intimidating. Today's SPC software programs were designed to plug in the correct formulas and perform the number crunching for you so instead you can spend your time effectively managing the process. Concentrate on understanding the situations presented here, and reach for the formulas on those rare occasions that you need to know *how* the data was derived.

Finally, Zontec has long maintained that quality is not just a function of the Quality Department. Everyone shares a stake in his or her organization's quality. By working as a team, quality becomes the natural way of doing business.

Here's to the process!

Richard K. Morris

The Book of Statistical Process Control

1.0 Introduction to SPC thinking

By a small sample we may judge the whole piece.
Miguel De Cervantes

1.1 Why SPC?

Success in the global market depends on quality. Companies that produce high quality consistently will succeed; those who do not will ultimately fail.

The emphasis here is on consistent high quality. It isn't enough to produce quality sporadically; one bad product can hurt a company's future sales. Inconsistent quality is also more expensive since bad parts have to be reworked or even scrapped. On the other hand, when quality improves productivity improves, costs drop, and sales go up.

Companies don't design poor quality; it is usually the result of a variation in some stage of production. Therefore, product quality depends on the ability to control the production process. This is where statistical process control, SPC, comes in. SPC uses statistics to detect variations in the process so they can be controlled.

This book offers a detailed look at SPC, from how and why it began to how it works. It also offers ways to start up an SPC program, and describes how to automate SPC.

1.2 Mass production and the need for standardization

Before the arrival of mass production, craftsmen managed every aspect of their products. They designed an item, produced its parts, and assembled them. They personally marketed their products and dealt directly with their customers.

If a problem came up, the craftsman could alter the product to prevent its recurrence or lose those customers who were unhappy with it. They had to balance the cost of production, the ease of subsequent operations, and customer standards as they saw fit. Thus, they had a good understanding of the overall picture.

This began to change in the late 1700's, when the United States had a shortage of skilled craftsmen and a need for a large quantity of muskets. Eli Whitney believed he could mass produce muskets, using machines to make parts that would be interchangeable with spares. These machines could be run by ordinary men, not skilled craftsmen. The government gave him a contract and funds, and he began to design and build the machines needed to make each part.

He recognized that if he relied on one machine, one small part out of order could make the whole machine useless. To avoid this, he developed separate processes for each part and designed a machine for each process. That way if an experiment showed one process fault, he could adopt another machine without changing the method. Along with the machines, he invented tools, gages, jigs, and fixtures so all the parts would be close to dimensional tolerances. He also trained his workers on how to use them.

When he did not deliver the muskets on time, some in the government questioned his methods and his ability to fulfill his contract. He responded by letting a group of his skeptics assemble muskets from a trunk of parts, using only screws and screwdrivers. They saw that the weapons could be assembled without the normal fitting and filing and granted him an extension. Although it took several years longer than he expected to deliver the first 10,000 muskets, he succeeded in developing a way to mass produce them.

Whitney succeeded because he knew that variation existed, and he adjusted his process to compensate for it. He knew that for mass production to work, his machines had to standardize the parts so they would be interchangeable. He knew that to be interchangeable each part had to fit the assembly without filing. This is why he developed gages representing the part the product had to fit.

Gages were a key to standardizing parts and craftsmen began to use them to judge their products. Now, instead of adjusting each part to fit a unique assembly, they adjusted parts to fit the gage. This removed them from the needs of the end user. The buyers had to "specify" their requirements, and craftsmen shifted their focus from the product's function to the customer's specifications. They no longer understood the big picture.

It was up to the customer to define user requirements, and the producers fought for the widest tolerances they could get. With suppliers trying to coax wider tolerances out of customers and customers trying to narrow them, producers focused on taking the maximum advantage of specifications. This shifted the focus away from quality and led to the idea that defective parts can't be avoided. Rather than looking for ways to reduce defects, both producers and consumers accepted them as a natural part of mass production. With only a few producers, consumers often had the choice of poor quality or nothing at all.

During World War II, the U.S. Government classified quality control as top secret and required all military suppliers to use control charts. When the war ended, the government relaxed its requirements and suppliers dropped the charts with other "red tape." They failed to recognize the power of statistical tools in predicting and controlling production processes. With the soaring demand for products, supplier efforts focused on how many instead of how good. There was little reason to improve quality.

However, in Japan it was a different story. Between 1945 and 1949, the Civil Communications Section of the Allied command upgraded the work practices of the Japanese by establishing quality standards and techniques. The Japanese had been inspecting for quality and knew their products lacked it. They also knew this inspection did not make their products any better. They began using statistics to control quality at the point of production and within a few decades became known as one of the highest quality producers in the world. The turning point for the Japanese was when they shifted from detecting poor quality to preventing poor quality.

The U.S. was forced to rethink its smug attitude toward quality when competition increased in the global market. With more selection, consumers could demand better quality. To stay competitive, producers had to shift their attention back to quality and they began working to continuously improve their products.

By the late 1970's, a number of overlapping and sometimes conflicting national quality system requirements emphasized the need for more uniform international guidelines. Within 10 years, the International Standards Organization (ISO), a worldwide federation representing nearly 100 countries, published the *ISO 9000 Standard Series*.

In general, ISO 9000 focuses the world's manufacturers on an agreed-upon level of quality in the delivery of goods and services. Certification to ISO 9000 indicates that a company understands, documents, implements and demonstrates the effectiveness of ISO-defined quality practices. Conformance with ISO 9000 is frequently a requirement in business-to-business purchasing transactions.

ISO 9000 guidelines are very generic allowing users wide latitude in how they establish their individual quality systems. SPC can be a powerful tool in achieving ISO 9000 certification by leading the way to observable process and quality improvement. On average, companies spend between three to nine months learning the standard requirements, training its personnel, developing and implementing compliant systems and monitoring their results.

Many industrial sectors have since realized the necessity to supplement the ISO quality system model with a set of requirements that satisfy internal, governmental, regulatory and global standards that apply only to them. The first of these was *Quality System Requirements QS-9000* for the U.S. auto industry, issued in 1994. A more globally focused standard, *ISO/TS 16949* now applies to automotive manufacturers worldwide.

Other supplemental industrial standards to ISO 9000 include *ISO 9100* for aerospace suppliers, *ISO 13485* for medical device manufacturers, and *TL 9000* for the telecommunications industry.

Though not a quality standard in the terms of ISO, a number of the major industrial nations have established awards programs for enterprises within their borders that are judged as the very best in quality. One of the most notable is the *Malcolm Baldrige National Quality Award* in the U.S., named for the late Secretary of Commerce whose managerial excellence contributed to long-term improvement and efficiency and effectiveness of the U.S. government.

Given annually, the Malcolm Baldrige Award bolsters the concept of quality improvement to small companies as well as large, to service industries as well as manufacturing and to the public sector as well as private enterprise.

1.3 What is quality?

Before we can control quality, we need to understand what the word "quality" means. Quality, like beauty, is in the eye of the beholder. Each of us judges the quality of many items every day, and we each have a different idea about what quality is for each item. We know what we like or what we want, and what we don't like or want. How we determine the quality of an item depends on both our personal preference and our frame of reference for that particular item.

For example, production workers might see quality as conformance to specifications. If the size of the hole they produce is within their tolerance, it is a good hole. If not, it's bad.

Marketing people might think of quality as something that sells well and causes little trouble for the customer.

Supervisors see quality when production is higher than normal and there are few reworks.

Customers see quality if the product does what they expect it to do without any breakdowns.

Quality is conformance to specification.
This idea comes from labeling parts that are in-spec as good and out-of-spec as bad. Are they really good and bad? No. Somebody has either

assigned or negotiated the tolerances and a simple stroke of a pen changing these tolerances can transform bad products into good.

Quality is a measure of how good a product is — quality is meeting customer acceptable quality levels. Does the quality of the product change when you renegotiate the contract with the customer? No, acceptable quality levels are simply tolerances on tolerances. They specify the number of times it is permissible to miss the target by a given amount.

Quality is zero defects.
This notion is based on our ability to define a defect. If we define a defect as a part out of spec, then we are right back at "conforming to the specifications."

Quality is the absence of variation.
This is a goal that initially sets many companies' SPC implementations in motion.

Quality is in the eyes of the beholder.
With manufactured products, quality is determined by the customer. If the customer thinks the quality is good, then it's good. In making the judgment the customer weighs competitive products, cost, performance, and personal preference.

Because we define a product's quality in relation to competing products, it is a constantly moving target. Finding this target means adjusting to meet the customer's needs as well as maintaining the competitive edge. This requires never-ending improvement.

Quality can be broken down into three areas of concern to the customer:

1) Design Quality
2) Manufacturing Quality
3) Performance Quality or Reliability

Design Quality is the intended shape, size, color and function of the product. The designer must assess the needs of the customer and select

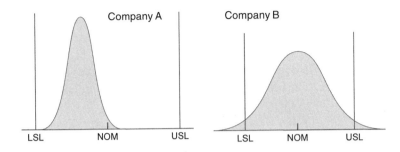

Figure 1.1
Distributions of output from two companies. All of Company A's product falls within specification limits. Company B's production is centered at the designed optimum, but does produce some out-of-spec parts.

characteristic values that will create the greatest customer satisfaction. Product quality can never be better than the quality of the design.

Manufacturing Quality is how well the product meets the design. It is this type of quality that is the subject of this book. The better the manufacturing quality is, the better the product quality will be. And if this type of quality is good, product quality will be more consistent. Keep in mind however, that while improving manufacturing will improve a product to a certain extent, it will never improve a poor design.

Performance Quality is a measure of how dependable a product is. The level of this type of quality is affected by how often a product fails, the time between failures, the time it takes to repair, and repair costs.

Most customers don't tell the manufacturer what they want directly. They tell them by buying or not buying. To stay competitive, a company must consider how their customers look at quality. From the customer's point of view, quality includes the marketing, engineering, manufacturing, and maintenance through which the product or service meets their expectations.

Figure 1.1 illustrates the output of two companies making the same part. Company A has much tighter control over the dimension but their process is centered near the low limit. Company B however doesn't have enough control to keep their products within spec all the time and produces a 3% out-of-spec product.

From a producer's point of view, Company A would appear to be the better company. The tighter control of the dimensions reduces the cost of materials.

A customer who is only buying one or two items would prefer Company B's product. Why? Company B produces an average of 68% of their product in the middle third of the tolerance. And chances are many of Company B's parts will be exactly on target — a perfect product. Company A's products run towards the low end of the limits, which means there is a slight chance of getting a perfect product and a good chance of getting an inferior one.

If Company A can center their process on the design target, they will have the better product. Centering a process is usually easier than reducing process variations. This is why controlling variables is the biggest problem in quality production.

1.4 Variation

If it was possible to make all items alike, we would not need tolerances. Since no two things are exactly alike, we must make allowances for the differences. Tolerances are these allowances. They provide a range over which a product can vary and still be accepted by the customer.

Of course, "accepted" is not "desired," and in the battle over width of tolerances the idea of a specific target has been lost. For example, ask almost any machinist what size a part is supposed to be, and you will get a range for an answer — "from 2.048 to 2.052 inches." Why isn't the answer "2.050 inches" if that is the target? Because with tolerances, we tend to aim for the acceptable range instead of the exact target. This means we are less likely to hit the target. It also means our variance will most likely be greater than if we aimed for the target.

Variance is a natural occurrence, but that doesn't mean we shouldn't try to control it. If we aim for a specific target value, instead of a range, we have more control of the variance. In archery, if you shoot for a bull's eye, your arrow is likely to land near it, but if you broaden your aim to encompass the entire target, your arrow could land any-where. The same is true for manufacturing.

A perfect product is one that is on target, so aiming for the target will improve product quality. Specifying a target value and controlling the variability makes more sense than focusing on tolerances.

1.5 Statistical thinking vs. Engineering thinking

Engineers have it made. In the world of engineering, two plus two always equals four. When products are designed the dimensions are exact, the calculations are accurate, and the resulting characteristics are known.

Manufacturing is not so precise. Variations can occur anywhere in the process and are often hard to predict accurately. People work with items that were intended to be two inches long, but in reality they are anywhere from an eighth of an inch too big to an eighth of an inch too small. Two plus two seldom equals four.

This has frustrated managers world-wide for a long time. Engineers predict the output of a process and we wonder why things didn't turn out as planned. The problem is in the definition of what should be.

Statisticians addressed this problem by developing methods for calculating expected results which take variation into account. Their methods call for observing the process in its actual environment so the expected variability can be measured.

1.6 Development of Shewhart control charts

In the 1930's, Walter Shewhart devised a way to predict what could happen during a production process. His technique involved collecting observations from the shop floor, running calculations on this data and then plotting it on a graph. Based on statistics of what had happened in the process, he could predict what would happen in the future.

Comparing the actual result to his prediction was a simple matter of plotting points on graph paper. His graphs became known as the Shewhart Control Charts. They were and are used to control the output of manufacturing processes.

1.7 Prevention vs. detection as quality control

Estimates show that it is ten times more costly to correct a problem than it is to prevent it. With this kind of savings, companies can reduce prices, expand their R&D, and increase profits at the same time.

Changes to a product's characteristics are merely a reflection of changes in input. Therefore, the key to preventing defects in a product is to monitor and control all aspects of its production.

1.8 Definition of a process

Most people think of a process as a machine or task, but it is more complex than that. A process is the entire system of machines, raw materials, people, procedures, environment, and measurements, used to make a product. Figure 1.2 illustrates this concept.

You can define a process to suit your needs. If your interest is the production of plastic buckets, you can define the process as the bucket, machine and the plastic. Or you can expand the definition to include all production in the plant as well as external factors that impact plant operations.

A process has inputs, actions, and outputs. Each input has a source or supplier and each output has a customer or a user.

A process is at the mercy of its inputs. If the input changes, the change reflected in the output. The most common way to deal with this is to change certain inputs to compensate for unwanted changes in others. However, since each factor can vary greatly, this method is time con-suming and costly. If you reduce changes or input variation, the pro-cess will need fewer corrections, the products will be more uniform, and less work will be needed to produce the same output. It is far more

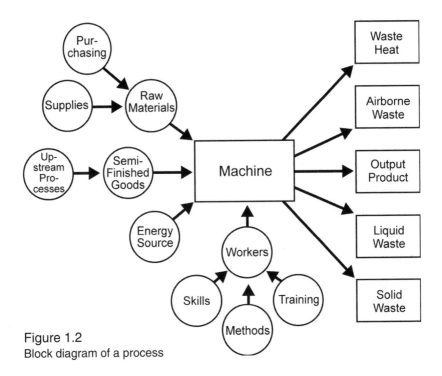

Figure 1.2
Block diagram of a process

effective to determine which inputs affect the process most, and control them, than to compensate for changes in these inputs.

1.9 Who is the customer?

Every process has customers. They are the people who receive the output of the process. They may be the next process in the plant or the people who buy the end product. The goals of a quality program are to define the customers for each process, and to make sure their needs are met. This is where the idea of specs clashes with our thinking. Rather than asking what the customer wants, specs ask what is the worst the customer will accept.

1.10 Determining loss

When we think of quality as meeting a target value, we need a way to calculate the loss incurred when we don't hit the target. If you use tolerances, loss is easy to determine. If we know the cost of labor and materials used to fix or replace bad items, we can estimate our loss due to poor quality.

In the past, companies only allocated poor quality costs to the parts that fell outside the spec limits, as shown in Figure 1.3. In this example, two parts are produced, X and Y. X is 0.005 inches inside the lower spec limit and Y is 0.005 inches outside this limit. X is good, Y is bad. The cost of poor quality for X is zero, while the cost for poor quality for Y is $20. Both parts are similar and both are very far from the target, yet there is a large difference in the cost. Although this method distributes the cost of poor quality, it does not depict the loss accurately.

A loss is actually a gradual change from good to worthless. Any movement away from the design target exerts some degree of loss. Variance must be compensated for, if not directly by the part maker, then by next department, the end producer, or the final buyer. It is the end producer who ultimately suffers the cost of variance— a loss of business, loss of sales, loss due to rework and repairs, etc. These losses eventually come full circle and cost the producer.

This is why long range thinkers consider the loss experienced by their customers as well as their own direct loss. They distribute costs of poor quality to every part that misses the design target. This method distributes costs progressively; the farther from the design target, the greater the cost.

Figure 1.4 shows this method of distributing poor quality losses. Instead of beginning where parts fall outside spec limits, losses begin at the point where the target is first missed.

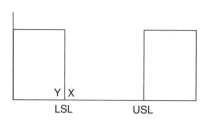

Figure 1.3
Traditional quality loss curve.

1.11 Common causes vs. special causes

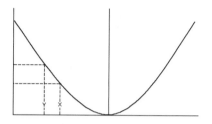

Figure 1.4
Continuous quality loss curve.

When he developed the control charts, Dr. Shewhart recognized that certain variations were a part of every process and he accounted for them in his predictions of future events. He called these sources of variation random or chance causes and found there was no one event that caused them. Now called common causes, these variations are measured and documented in control charts.

Not all variation is built into the system. Some variations have identifiable causes such as human error, bad raw materials, or equipment failure. Known as *assignable* or *special causes*, these are the sources of variation that control charts are designed to signal. Assignable causes interfere with the process so it produces an irregular output. Control charts reflect this disturbance, allowing the problem to be tracked down.

1.12 What to control?

With process control, the focus is on the process inputs and the output seems unimportant. The reason for this is that the output can't be changed directly. Only the inputs can be directly changed and these changes must be controlled. The quality of the final output depends entirely on the inputs.

The output does provide information about process capability for the customer's point of view. It also helps to determine which inputs have a significant effect on the process results. Controlling of the process comes once these inputs are identified and direct controls are set up for them.

1.13 Human elements of SPC programs

SPC alone will not improve quality. Statistics can only show where problems are, it can't solve them. It is up to people to prevent and solve process problems. Since management can't be everywhere solving every problem, workers must have the training, motivation, and authority to deal with everyday variance.

It's one thing to show a person how to operate a machine and another thing to train them. Training is teaching workers about potential problems, and how to resolve and prevent them as well as how to run equipment. When you add the authority to resolve problems to thorough training, you build confidence, increase motivation, and improve productivity.

Motivation also comes from feedback about their work and from knowing how the results of their labor affects the next step and the final output. Asking for efforts that have no immediate feedback runs against the grain of people who have been rewarded their entire life for the results of this shift, this week, this month, this quarter, or this year. Not knowing the results of their work is not only demoralizing, it also reduces productivity and increases the potential for errors.

Take, for example, the game of bowling. Thousands of people pay money to bowl every week because it's fun. They roll the ball, watch the pins fly, and instantly know how well they did. Now let's change the game slightly to reflect the environment many workers find themselves in.

We'll hang a bed sheet across the lanes about ten feet past the foul line. This sheet completely blocks the bowler's view of the pins. We'll also remove score sheets and scoring equipment. The foul line light and buzzer will be disabled, but we'll still count fouls in the usual way.

After being trained by the team captain, the bowler rolls the ball and sits down. It may have been a strike or it may have been a gutter ball. There is no feedback, so who knows? Would bowling still be fun? Of course not.

You say workers do have feedback—they receive monthly accounting reports of scrap and rework charges. OK, we'll mail the bowlers their scores once a month. Is that any better?

Some supervisors provide feedback to workers when they make an error. We'll add this into our game of bowling by having the pin boy holler, "You messed up that time," whenever he notices a poor roll. But since he is so busy, this only happens a couple of times a night.

In a situation like this, the scores would not be very good. Yet workers are often expected to shoot for goals they are told exist but are given no way to measure their success.

SPC removes the sheet and provides a means of keeping score. The effects of actions become measurable and provide feedback.

Workers are likely to complain about the perceived extra work that an SPC program requires. In the past, operators made the product and someone else checked it. Now, to tighten process control and provide more timely feedback, the person who does the work is also responsible for checking it. This new work does cut into piecework, and if an incentive system is in place, the bonus is affected. However, this is only true in the initial stages of the program when old practices are still followed and the charts are first introduced. As workers make changes in the process, they are able to streamline their efforts, reduce the number of reworks, and increase their productivity.

Like bowling, work is more enjoyable when you can see the results. Morale will most likely increase as SPC is implemented. As morale improves, workers take more pride in their work. More pride improves product quality. This leads to the chain reaction taught by W. Edwards Deming, in which improved quality improves efficiency and decreases costs. Better products and lower prices increase sales and product demand, which in turn creates more jobs. Making workers a part of the quality equation can only improve product output and sales.

1.14   Management's responsibilities

Statistical process control provides management insight into what is actually happening on the production floor. In our bowling example, removing the sheet from the lanes is the job of the manager of the facility, not the bowler. Likewise, the job of company management is to adjust the rules of the game so workers can make the best use of their skills. While there are certain adjustments workers can make, most improvement comes from changes only management can make. Management must set the stage for workers to do their best work.

Managers do not try to inhibit workers' performance. Although they are not as close to the process, they often suffer from the same lack of feedback as the workers. Workers and management must work together to identify and document factors that make the job more difficult, change them, and measure the effectiveness of these changes.

If workers use SPC or other techniques to identify problem areas and management doesn't act on these problems, worker support for the program will fade.

1.15   Team approach to problem solving

Solving problems usually affects other processes up or down stream. Remember the early craftsman? Each step he made affected other processes, but he had the responsibility for these and hence could deal with the reactions down the line himself. Today, it is important to include everyone whom the solution could affect in the problem resolution, and to do so in the early stages.

1.16   Negative effects of specs and work quotas

A company that constantly seeks ways to improve its production process will be healthy. In our competitive market, if we wait for the customer to demand improved products we will fall behind. Aiming for spec limits or to achieve a quota is the same as setting a goal; once you reach it there is no reason to go further.

Let's say your process produces 5% out of spec parts, and each part costs $10 to repair or rework. If monthly production is 1000 parts, the cost of rework is $500. You would probably let an engineer spend a few thousand dollars to improve this process.

Once the production falls within the spec limits, there is no need to spend money on improving the process under the traditional loss system. That is, until the competition starts selling parts with a tighter distribution. One reaction is to narrow the "internal" specs so you only ship out the parts that are equally good. However, this would increase reworks and associated costs.

Now let's look at a work quota system. Assume workers have a quota of 800 parts per shift. Suppose you dock them for each part short of the quota and give them a bonus for each part over the 800. The primary goal is to make 800+ parts, and all efforts are to increase production speed. Quality slows them down, so it falls by the wayside. In this situation, you're not only encouraging poor quality work, you're paying extra for it.

Any type of formal rules or requirements fosters the "how can I beat the system" type of thinking. Management tries to design rules that make personal goals mesh with company goals. This is fine until business conditions change and the rules no longer reflect the company's needs. Raw material price and availability change, energy prices change, technology changes, customer demands change. As a result, strict systems of measuring work are less effective and often hinder productivity.

2.0　Statistical distributions

To measure is to know.

James Clerk Maxwell

2.1　Why do we need statistics?

Chapter 1 looked at the effects of variation on production and why we should control it. We also discussed how we can use statistics to measure and track variance. Statistics make it possible for us to make fairly accurate predictions with just small groups of data. It is not possible to predict individual events with statistics, but they will give you an insight to the overall results.

For example, no one can predict how long a person will live. An accident or illness could happen tomorrow, or the person may live to be 100 years old. Life insurance companies, however, can accurately predict what percent of the population will live to be 50, 60, 70 and beyond. This is the type of information that we need about our production process.

Statistics let us make estimates without knowing all the possible results. For example, no one has measured all the people in the United States, but we know the average height. We find the average by sampling a small part of the population and applying what we learn from it to the whole population.

Statistics deals with two areas: the past and the future. We use statistics to summarize past events so we can understand them. We then use this summary to make predictions about the future. SPC applies this to process control allowing us to predict the future course of the process and its output based on what has happened in the past.

To understand how SPC works, you'll need to know some basic statistical concepts. This chapter presents an overview of these concepts.

2.2 Populations

In statistics, a population or universe is the entire group of subjects in a study. A population can be anything—people, screws, all parts made by one machine, etc. To learn about a population, we study the distribution of specific features throughout the group. The shape of the distribution tells us if the group has certain tendencies: if it's balanced, for example. We use these tendencies to make predictions about future events.

We'll look at some common distributions and what they reveal later in this chapter.

2.3 Probability

Statistics is about probability, which is the chance that something will happen. We want to know the odds of an event occurring or how often it will occur.

For example, a coin has two sides, so there are two possible results when it is flipped: "heads" or "tails." If you flip it, there is a 50% or 1:2 chance that heads will appear.

These odds tell us how likely our predictions are to happen. SPC uses probability to predict how likely a specific result will happen again.

2.4 Statistical symbols

We use symbols to write statistical results in an easy form. For example, we use 'x' to represent each reading or observation in a sample. If there is more than one reading, we use subscripts to identify which reading we're referring to. For example, 'x_1' is the first reading, 'x_2' is the second. When we refer to a specific reading, but don't want to give it an exact value, we use the notation 'x_i' and say it is the ith reading.

We use 'n' to represent the number of readings in one sample (sometimes called a subgroup), and 'N' for the the number of readings taken in the study. For the number of samples in the study, we use 'k'.

If we have 25 samples of five readings each, we have a total of 125 observations. The equation looks like this:

$$n = 5, k = 25$$
$$N = n \times k = 5 \times 25 = 125$$

When we sample from a population, we make calculations using the data we collected. These calculations allow us to narrow the data from many sample readings into one value. These single values derived from the sampled data are statistics. Each calculated value is a statistic, and each statistic is an estimate for the true population values.

If we look at a deck of cards, the values range from one to thirteen, if Jacks are 11, Queens 12 and Kings 13. The distribution mean or expected value (also called the average) of the possible values is seven:

$$(1+2+3+4+5+6+7+8+9+10+11+12+13) / 13 = 7$$

Suppose we select three cards at random: 3, 7 and a Queen. The sample average would be 7.333. If the cards we selected were 4, 6 and an Ace, the sample average would be 3.667. We would not expect each sample to have the same sample average nor equal exactly seven. Sample statistics are only at best an estimate of the true population values.

You can create statistics using any method you want to use on your sample data. Each statistic has its own variability with repeated samplings and therefore, its own distribution. We can predict how each statistic will behave if we understand this distribution. Any changes we see in the distribution of our statistic will reflect changes in the readings the statistic was calculated from. If we monitor the behavior of the statistics, we can monitor the behavior of the process.

2.5 Measures of central tendency

There are several statistics we can calculate for a distribution, so we can compare it to other distributions or describe it for others. One such statistic is the middle of the distribution or the central tendency. We have four ways to measure central tendency:

Finding the *mid-range* value or the *midpoint* of the range is one way to find the center of the distribution.

We find the highest and lowest value and say the center of the distribution is mid-way between the two. It is calculated by adding the highest and lowest values and dividing this sum by two. If you use this statistic, keep in mind that extreme values affect it, and it doesn't reflect any values in between them. If, for example, you draw 15 cards from a deck: 3, 4, 5, 6, 7, 8, 5, 4, 9, 9, 4, 10, 7, Queen (12) and 4, the highest card is 12 and the lowest is 3. The mid-range for these 15 cards is 7.5 as shown in Figure 2.1A.

The second way to describe the center of the distribution is to find the *mode*. The mode is the value that occurs most often in the sample. Although the mode can be applied to raw data, it is usually used for grouped data, such as data for histograms. The mode tells us which value occurs most often, but doesn't show a relationship to other values. For example, if you looked at the same 15 cards we found the range for, you'd find the mode of these cards is 4. This is shown in Figure 2.1B.

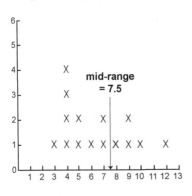

Figure 2.1A
Mid-range

Finding the *median* is the third way to describe the central tendency. The median is the value that has

50% of the values on either side of it. To find it, we must sort the data into ascending or descending order, and then count off half of the readings from either end. If there is an odd number of readings, there will be an exact middle value. If the number of readings is even, the median will fall between the two numbers, and we must average them to find it. As shown in Figure 2.1C, the median value of our 15 cards is 6.

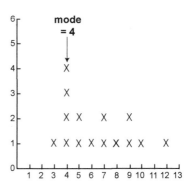

Figure 2.1B
Mode

The *median* shows the relative position of the data with respect to one another, but order is all it responds to. If half of the data spreads out more than the other half, the median doesn't show it.

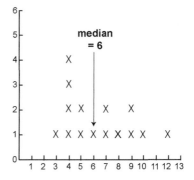

Figure 2.1C
Median

The fourth way to measure central tendency is to find the *average* or *mean*. To find the average of a series of samples, add the sample values and divide this sum by the total number of samples. An 'X' with a line over it ($\overline{X}$) symbolizes the average and is read as X-bar. The average not only shows changes in the relative order of the data, but it also reflects changes in the distances between data values. The average value for our example is 6.47, as shown in Figure 2.1D.

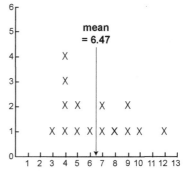

Figure 2.1D
Mean

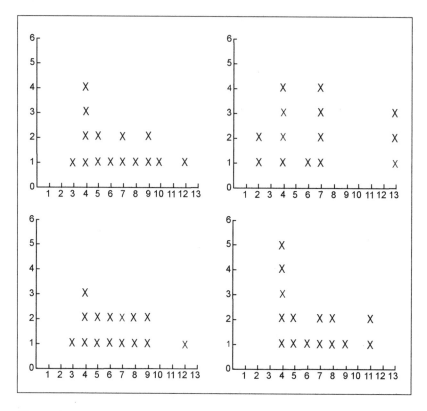

Figure 2.2
Four processes with the same central tendency values, but with very different dispersions

As you can see, we have four different central tendency values for our sample. Each measure of central tendency tells us something different about our sample. The mean tells us the average of the sample, but it can't tell us which value occurred most often, and not the relative position of the values. We can use each measure of central tendency to compare samples; however, samples can have the same central tendency values, but differ greatly, as shown in Figure 2.2.

Each of these four samples has a mode = 4, a median = 6, a mid-range = 7.5 and a mean 6.47, but as you can see, how the values spread out is quite different. This is why we also need to determine the spread when we compare distributions.

2.6 Measures of process dispersion

We just looked at an example of how distributions can have the same central tendency values and yet be very different. We call this spread process dispersion. We use process dispersion values with central tendency values for a more complete description of our data.

Range is the easiest way to describe the spread of data. To find the range, subtract the minimum value from the maximum value. The larger the range, the greater the spread of values. Like the mid-range, the range only takes the two extremes into account. For the card sample: 3, 4, 5, 6, 7, 8, 5, 4, 9, 9, 4, 10, 7, 12 and 4, the range is 9. 'R' is the symbol for range.

To include other values in our analysis we calculate the average value, find the distance each value is from the average, and total these distances. Since adding positive and negative values can give us a total of zero, we add the absolute values of the distances be-tween the average of the group of data and each value. (For the absolute value, just ignore the negative sign is there is one.) Then divide this total by the number of readings in the group to get the average distance from the center value. This statistic is the *Mean Absolute Deviation*, or MAD. Its formula is:

$$\text{MAD} = \frac{X_i - \overline{X}}{n} \quad \text{or} \quad \frac{X_i - \overline{X} + X_2 - \overline{X} + \ldots X_n - \overline{X}}{n}$$

If we take our cards again with the mean equal to 6.47, the MAD would be calculated as:

Observation	Deviation
3	3.47
4	2.47
4	2.47
4	2.47
4	2.47
5	1.47
5	1.47
6	0.47
7	0.53
7	0.53
8	1.53
9	2.53
9	2.53
10	3.53
12	5.53

$$33.47 / 15 = 2.23 = MAD$$

There are two other measures of spread that are important in SPC. They are the standard deviation and the variance.

Finding the standard deviation is similar to the way we find the MAD, but instead of using the absolute values, we find the square of the difference, and divide it by the number of samples. The standard deviation is the square root of that value. Either an 's' or σ (sigma) can symbolize the standard deviation. Its formula is:

$$\sigma = \sqrt{\frac{(X_i - X)^2}{n}}$$

Looking at our card values again, the standard deviation would be calculated as:

Observation	Deviation	Sq. of Deviation
3	3.47	12.0409
4	2.47	6.1009
4	2.47	6.1009
4	2.47	6.1009
4	2.47	6.1009
5	1.47	2.1609
5	1.47	2.1609
6	0.47	0.2209
7	0.53	0.2809
7	0.53	0.2809
8	1.53	2.3409
9	2.53	6.4009
9	2.53	6.4009
10	3.53	12.4609
12	5.53	30.5809
		99.7335

$$\sqrt{99.7335 / 15} = \sqrt{6.6489} = 2.5786 = \sigma$$

For some calculations you'll find the standard deviation squared is easier to work with. This statistic is called the variance, and is denoted by 's²' or σ^2 (sigma squared). Its equation is:

$$\sigma^2 = \frac{(X_i - X)^2}{n}$$

If you know the standard deviation, just square it for the variance. (Or don't take the square root.) For our card values, the standard deviation is 2.5786 so the variance is 6.649.

2.7 Some common distributions

The behavior of most data can be described by the following distributions. Each of these has different properties and will not only reveal specific information about the data, but also will help you make inferences about the whole population.

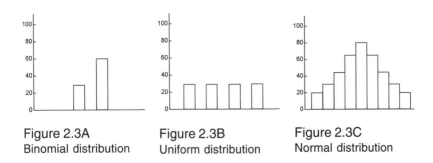

Figure 2.3A
Binomial distribution

Figure 2.3B
Uniform distribution

Figure 2.3C
Normal distribution

The simplest one of these is the *binomial distribution*, which is a probability distribution. It reflects events that have only two possible outcomes. For example, if you flip a coin, the "heads" or "tails" outcomes create a binomial distribution, as does calling a part good or bad. The possibility of one or the other outcome is equal. Take the coin, for example; each time you flip it, the chance that it will be "heads" or "tails" is the same. The same is true if you label each part as defective. Figure 2.3A shows a binomial distribution.

When each possible outcome has an equal chance of happening, the distribution is said to be *uniform*, or rectangular. An example of this is rolling a fair die; each value has the same chance of occurring. A prominent feature of the uniform distribution is its symmetry, as shown in Figure 2.3B. Along with the symmetry, you need to know the mean and the standard deviation to describe this distribution.

The *normal distribution* is also symmetrical. With this distribution, the likelihood of an event occurring increases as the values move toward the center or mean value, and tail off again once they've moved beyond the mean. If the data has a normal distribution, as shown in Figure 2.3C, it will show the familar bell-shape curve when plotted on a chart.

Normal distributions occur most often with measured data, such as the height of people in the U.S. or time it takes to add a given amount of a reagent to a vat. They occur naturally when the data comes from a stable process. The normal distribution also requires

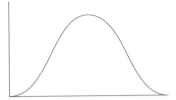

Figure 2.3D
Normal curve

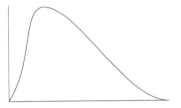

Figure 2.3E
Poisson distribution

the mean and standard deviation to describe it. The normal distribution is a symmetical distribution, meaning that both sides of the mean take the same shape.

Suppose we draw another 15 cards: 3, 4, 5, 5, 6, 7, 7, 7, 7, 8, 8, 9, 9, 10, 11. The mean, median and mode are all 7, so the distribution is normal and creates a normal curve as shown in Figure 2.3D. Like the uniform distribution, we can describe it using the mean and standard deviation.

A fourth type of distribution is the *Poisson distribution*, which gets its name from Simeon Poisson who first described it. It is used to describe details, where the probability that a specific event will occur is small and the number of trials is large. For example, you could use a Poisson distribution to describe the number of cars that go through an intersection during rush hour every day. You always begin this distribution with zero, and you only need the mean to fully describe it. Figure 2.3E shows this type of distribution.

2.8 Properties of the normal curve

Because sample averages have the tendency to become normal, the normal curve is at the heart of SPC. If we have a process with a normal distribution, we can make certain assumptions about the data based on the properties of a normal curve. Figure 2.4 shows a normal curve. When you look at this figure, you'll notice there are three sections under the curve that are marked off with percentages. Each of these sections is an equal distance on either side of the

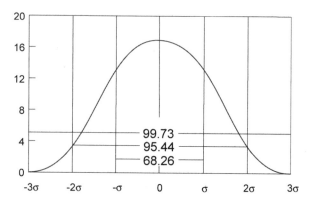

Figure 2.4
A normal curve
showing the
percent of data
that will fall into
each range of
standard
deviation

average value.   The distances represent multiples of one standard
deviation of the population and are labeled as σ, 2σ, etc.   No matter
what the average and standard deviation values are, every normal
curve will have these sections with the same percentages.

As you can see, about two thirds of the data, 68.26%, falls within
one standard deviation on either side of the mean.   If you move out
two standard deviations, you'll find 95.44% of the data, three standard deviations, 99.73% of the data, and six standard deviations,
99.99% of the data.   For practical purposes, we say the whole population falls between plus and minus three standard deviations.   This
is because out of 1,000 readings, only three will fall outside this

2.9   Central limit theorem

Each process behaves in its own way and will rarely fit one of the
classic statistical distributions exactly.   However, there is a law that
lets us use normal distribution to control the sample averages,
regardless of how individual samples are distributed.   It lets us
control the behavior of the process.

This law is the *Central Limit Theorem* and it states that regardless of
the shape of a universe's distribution, the distribution of the averages of the sample size n taken from that universe will move toward
a normal distribution as the sample size (n) grows.

In other words, no matter how samples are currently distributed, when the sample size grows, the distribution of the sample averages will approach normal.

You also will notice there is less variability in the sample averages as the sample size (n) increases. If we go back to the deck of cards and draw only sets of two from the deck, the average of each set will vary greatly. We could draw a King and a ten, or a one and a four. If we draw ten cards, the average will be much closer to the true average of seven.

With this law there is no need for concern about the distribution of individual readings for process control purposes.

The central limit theorem lets us quantify this shrinking of the variability. How much the standard deviation of the sample averages shrinks as the sample size (n) increases is equal to:

$$\frac{\sigma\,(\overline{X})}{\sqrt{n}}$$

We use this formula to estimate the standard deviation of a population if we know the standard deviation of the sample averages and the sample size. We'll look at ways to apply this to the production environment in later chapters.

3.0 Data collection & recording

If you can't measure it, you can't manage it.

Anonymous

An SPC program is only as good as its data. Data can point out problems, tell you their causes, and how often they happen. Data can show you much variation is in the process, and when the process is out of control. It can lay the groundwork for action.

To do all this, it has to be the right kind of data for your purpose. It has to represent the population it is supposed to represent, and it has to be organized. If the data fails these criteria, it can lead you to the wrong conclusions and the wrong type of action.

3.1 Types of data

The types of data most common in SPC are *variable* and *attribute*. Data falls into one of these groups based on the way it's collected. Variables are data that's measured, such as length, weight, temperature and diameter. They can be any whole number or fraction, such as 1½ inches, 1.342 pounds, 0.0003 centimeters, 5 degrees or 3 feet.

Attributes are counted data, such as the number of defects. They are often a record of go/no-go, pass/fail or yes/no. Because they are tallies, they must be whole numbers such as 1, 154, 68, etc. Either the part has a defect or it does not. You would not record a half of a tally. The attribute value would be the total number of tallies. You can also classify data in either of these groups by its purpose. This includes data for analysis, regulation, process control and acceptance or rejection.

Data for analysis
This type of data is used to study past results, make new tests and to study the relationship between causes and their effects.

Data for acceptance of rejection
This is point-of-inspection, go/no-go data.

Data for regulation
This type of data is used to adjust the process, and calls for direct action, such as temperature changes.

Data for process control
This type of data shows if the process is in or out of control, and shows process trends.

3.2 Characteristics

To control the process, we need to collect, analyze and act on data from the characteristics that make up both the process and the part. A characteristic is a feature of a part or its process, such as the dimensions, speed, hardness, smoothness, flatness and weight.

Before you can collect data, decide which characteristics are most important for improving your product quality. Keep in mind that you may change characteristics at any time. Once you've brought these characteristics under control so they're consistently producing the output you want, you may want to improve overall quality by controlling other characteristics.

When you look at each characteristic, consider the type of data you can get from it; how you'll measure it; and at what point of the process you'll measure it. You'll also want to know if the results can be proven, what can be learned from the data, and if you can act on it.

3.3 Collecting data

Before you begin collecting data, you have to determine what the purpose is. Is it to control the process, correct a problem or analyze the process? The purpose points the way to the kind of data you'll need, where to collect it, and how to organize it.

After identifying the purpose, you'll need to decide the extent and the objectives of the study. Then decide what type of data you'll need from which characteristics. Keep in mind that it isn't enough just to collect data. To reach a conclusion, you need to understand it. Therefore, you need to know how to analyze the data and what data will make the analysis accurate before collecting it. It is equally important to decide how you will collect the data. Consider what collection method will most clearly show the problem's cause or the process trends, etc.

Sampling
Since it's seldom feasible to test every item in a group, most studies are based on random samples. How we sample our universe determines our view of it, so the samples must be random. If they aren't we won't have an accurate picture of the universe. The only way to insure random sampling is to develop a plan for sampling the data before we begin to collect it.

With sampling, we collect data on a number of items in the group, and apply the results of this study to the whole group. When our plan is solid with enough truly random samples, the results of our study will accurately reflect the whole group.

There are several things to consider when you develop a sampling plan. The goal of sampling is to get information that accurately reflects your population. First identify what needs to be controlled, then decide what sampling method to use, how often to take them, where they should come from, and how many will represent the group. For some studies, when to take a sample or the production order may be important. For example, if you wish to detect a change that won't last very long, the time between samples should be short. You'll also need to consider bias in the sampling and design a plan to avoid it.

The sampling method you use depends on the type of data you need. For attribute data, samples are lot-by-lot. Samples from each group are inspected and defects are tallied. Variable data comes from continuous process samples. This type of sampling involves taking measurements of random items in the process as it is running.

How often you take samples depends on what you are studying. For attributes, you'll probably take samples for each lot. For variables, you'll want to consider the nature of the process as well as the purpose of the study. You may need to take a sample every five minutes, hourly, daily or during each shift. The goal is to take samples often enough to get an accurate picture for your study.

Where the samples come from refers to the point in the process where the measurements are taken. Again, the purpose of your study determines this. For a count of the defects, the samples will be post-production. For variable data, where the samples come from depends on what data will reveal the most information about the process. This depends on the purpose, the characteristic, and the process. If your sample consists of readings of consecutive parts, it captures that specific time in the process. If you only need a summary of events over time, the readings can be from random parts. You would also use random sampling for readings from a chemical process.

The group of samples taken from a population must have all the characteristics that are in that population. Therefore, how many samples you take depends on how many will give you an accurate picture of the population.

In a random sample, every item in the population has an equal chance of being taken. In a biased sample, every item doesn't have an equal chance. Only taking the items you can easily reach will give you a biased sample. So will selecting only those with obvious defects. If the bias is small, you can still get an accurate picture of the population, but there is no way to know the amount of bias. Design your sampling plans to avoid bias.

Sample Size

When developing a sampling plan, you must also decide how many readings to take for each sample. The number of readings, or sample size, determines how much variation the control chart will reflect. An increase in the sample size causes a decrease in the variation between samples. Thus, an X-bar chart with n = 5 shows less variation between samples than one with n = 2. A sample size increase also increases variation within a sample. This is shown in the range chart.

In an X-bar chart, variation decreases as the sample size increases. Because there is less variation, the control limits are tighter. Tighter control limits make the chart more sensitive. Points outside the limits on a chart with n = 5 may be within the limits of n = 2. Figure 3.1 shows four X-bar charts created with the same data. For chart 1, n = 1; for chart 2, n = 3; for chart 3, n = 5; and for chart 4, n = 10. Each chart has the same scale, so you can easily see the difference in control limits as the sample size increases.

As the sample size increases through five, the range between samples decreases. For samples larger than five, the variance between samples is more consistent. Because it levels off, you seldom need more than five readings in a sample. For example, the second column of Table 3.1 shows 24 samples. In this column n = 1, and values range from 18 - 25. Using the same readings and a sample size of two, the samples run from 18.5 - 22.5.

When first bringing a process under control, use a small sample size, such as two, and take samples frequently. This way, the chart will show some out-of-control points, but not enough to overwhelm you. If a majority of the samples are outside the limits, cut the sample size. Once you've eliminated the causes of the outside points and stabilized the process, you can increase the sample size to find more variation. As you tighten the control limits and eliminate the problem causes, you improve your process. This should be a continuous cycle.

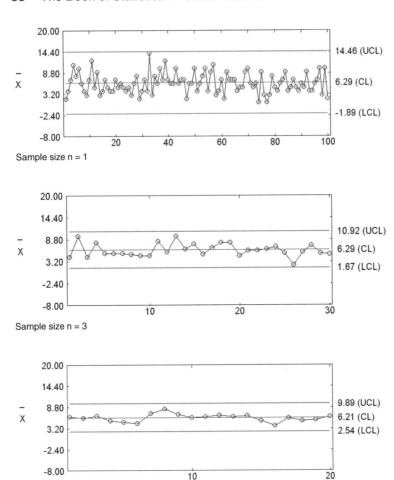

Sample size n = 1

Sample size n = 3

Sample size n = 5

Sample size n = 10

Figure 3.1
X-bar charts with the same measurements, but different sample sizes

n=	1	2	3	4	5	6	7	8
1	19.0	21.0	21.0	21.0	20.8	20.5	20.7	21.0
2	23.0	21.0	20.0	21.0	20.6	20.8	20.4	20.2
3	21.0	19.5	21.0	20.0	19.8	21.0	20.6	20.5
4	21.0	22.5	20.7	20.3	21.0	19.8	+	
5	20.0	19.5	20.5	+				
6	19.0	20.5	22.7	20.5				
7	22.0	20.0	19.4					
8	23.0	20.5	20.4					
9	18.0	22.5						
10	21.0	18.5						
11	19.0	19.5						
12	22.0	21.5						
13	20.0							
14	20.0							
15	18.0							
16	23.0							
17	25.0							
18	20.0							
19	19.0							
20	18.0							
21	21.0							
22	18.0							
23	20.0							
24	23.0							

Table 3.1

3.4 Recording data

You can collect all the data in the world, but if you can't understand it, it's useless. The key to understanding data is to organize it. It is best to do this as you collect it so you're sure you've collected all the pertinent information.

Some SPC software packages can take readings directly from gages and organize the data for you as it comes in. However, if you can't set up direct gage input for the information you need, check sheets are a good way to organize the data manually. For the best results, plan how you'll record the data and develop the check sheet before you begin to collect the data.

Along with helping you organize data, check sheets remind the user to record all the information the study needs. They should be as simple to use as possible so there are few errors in recording the data.

There are different check sheets for different purposes and types of data. For variable data, there are check sheets for measured data and distribution. For attribute data, there are check sheets to record how many defects of each type, causes, and where the defects are located. You also can create a check sheet to verify the final inspection.

Regardless of the type of check sheet your study requires, you'll want to include spaces for the study identification, the date, shift, method of collecting, where the data came from, and who collected it. Check sheets for variable data should include machine and gage IDs, the time the sample was taken and how often they are to be taken. You may also want to include the spec limits, so you'll know right away if this process is out of spec. All check sheets should have plenty of space for the data and notes.

Check Sheets for Measured Data
Check sheets for measured data provide a way to record and organize variable data. Along with the basic check sheet information, they contain a record of each measurement in a series of samples, and the average and range for each series. As mentioned, they should include the specific machine, gage, and the time of the readings, as well as a space for notes. A sample check sheet for measured data appears in Figure 3.2.

Check Sheets for Distribution
Another way to record variable data is with a check sheet for distribution. These show how frequently each measurement occurs. This type of study normally has a set time period which should appear somewhere on the check sheet. These check sheets contain a grid with the specific dimensions listed on one axis. The other axis represents the frequency of each value. This check sheet also should include room for totaling the frequency of each value. Figure 3.3 shows a sample check sheet for distribution.

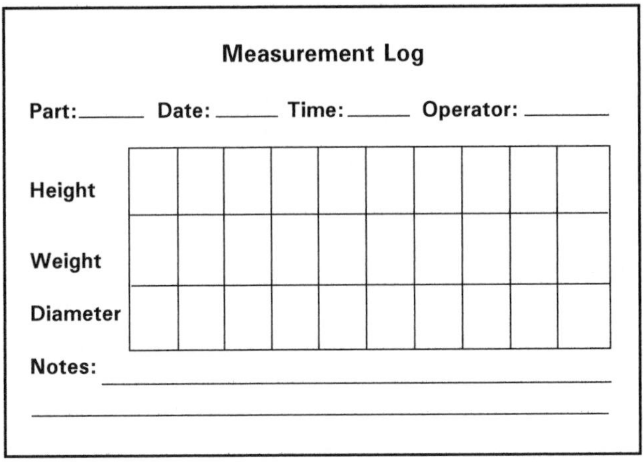

Measurement Log

Part:_____ Date: _____ Time: _____ Operator: _____

Height

Weight

Diameter

Notes: _____

_____

Figure 3.2
Check sheet for measured data

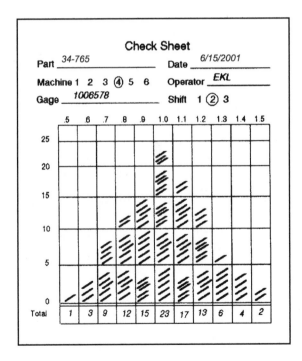

Figure 3.3
Check sheet for distribution

Check Sheet for Defects

Part No: 13547 Lot No: 35B Date: 5-18-2001
Shift: 3 Inspector: Frank Russell
Production Stage: Mid-point
Remarks: Irregular tool vibration increased number of scratches

Type	Count	Total	%
Puncture	~~IIII~~ III	8	14
Scratch	~~IIII~~ ~~IIII~~ ~~IIII~~ ~~IIII~~ II	22	41
Dent	III	3	6
Crack	~~IIII~~ ~~IIII~~	10	19
Other	~~IIII~~ ~~IIII~~ I	11	20
Total Defects: 54			

Figure 3.4
Defect check sheet

		Monday			Tuesday			Wednesday			Thursday			Friday		
Machine	Operator	1	2	3	1	2	3	1	2	3	1	2	3	1	2	3
1	A	ΔΔΘ X●■	ΔΘΘ X●	ΔΘX X■	ΘX●	ΔΘX	ΔX● X■● Θ■	●ΘΔ ■■■ Θ	■XΘ Δ	ΔΘX	ΘXX Δ■	ΘX● Δ	XX■	ΘX●	ΔX	■■
	B	ΘXX Δ●■	ΔΘX	ΔΔΘ X■■ Δ	●XΔ	●■	ΔΔΔ ΔX■	ΔΘX ●	●XΘ ●●Δ ■	ΔΔΘ	Δ■	XXΔ ●●Δ	ΔΔΔ ΔΘ■	ΔX●	ΔXX ●■Δ	ΔΔΘ ●●Δ
	C	ΔΘ■	XXX XXX	ΔXX X●	XXX XXX	Δ●●	X●■ ■	XXX X■■ ■	X	ΔX●	●●X	Δ●● ■	X	ΔXX ●	XXX XX●	X
2	A	ΔX● Θ●● Δ	ΘX● ●●■ ●■Δ	ΔX■	ΔΘX ●	ΘX● Δ	XXΔ ●●Θ Δ●●	ΔΘΔ ■	●ΘΔ ■	XXΔ	ΔΘX	ΔX●	ΔΘX	ΔX●		Θ■
	B	ΔΘ●	X●Δ	XXX ●Δ	XΔ● ●ΔX	■■	X●● Δ	Δ●■	●	ΔXΔ	Δ●Δ X■	X●● Δ	ΔXX	Δ●	Δ●	ΔXX
	C	XΘΔ X●X	X●Δ	XΔΔ ●■■	Δ●Δ XX■		ΔX●	XXX XXX		ΔX●	XXX X	XX●Δ	■	XΔX ●X■	ΔX	Δ■■
3	A	ΔΘX ■	ΘX● X●● ΘΔ	ΔX■	ΔΔ●	Δ●● ■■■ ●●Δ	ΔΔX ■	ΔXX	X●X● ●●■ Δ	●XΔ ●■● Δ	X●Δ ■■■ ■Δ	ΔX■	Δ●● ●■■ Δ■	■Δ●	ΔXX ■	Δ■
	B	ΔΘX ●■	ΘX● Δ	ΔX● Θ■	ΔΘ● ■■■ ●■Δ	ΘΔΔ ■■■ ΔX	ΔΔΘ	XX●	ΘX● ■ Δ	Θ	ΔΔ●		Δ●	ΔΔΔ	Θ●Δ	Θ■
	C	ΘΘX ■■■ ●ΘΔ	ΘΔΔ	ΘΘΘ Θ	ΔΘX	Θ●Δ	ΘΘ●	■	ΘΔΔ	●Δ Δ●Θ Δ●	ΔΘΘ X■	●ΘΔ ■■	ΘΘΘ	XΘΔ ■	Θ●■ Δ	ΔΘΘ ■

Defect Code: Scratch = Δ Puncture = Θ Dent = X Crack = ● Other = ■

Figure 3.5
Check sheet for causes

Check Sheets for Defects

Check sheets for defects contain a list of every defect type and space for tallying their occurrence. Most include a column for totals and one for percentages. This type of check sheet won't show you when a defect occurs, but will show you how often it happens. It also shows you which defect occurs most often, helping you decide which one to tackle first. Figure 3.4 shows a sample check sheet for defects.

Check Sheets for Causes

A check sheet for causes can reveal the relationship between defects and their causes. In this case, the check sheet is arranged to show machines, workers, defects, date and time as shown in Figure 3.5. These check sheets help you narrow down defect causes by showing you which defects happen most often, when they were most frequent, who produced them, and on what machine.

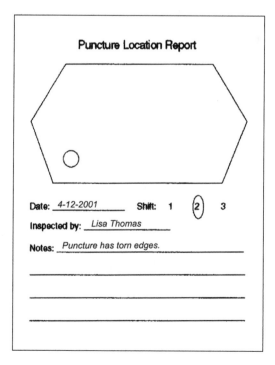

Check Sheets for Location

When you want to determine if a defect consistently occurs in the same place, use a check sheet for location. This type of check sheet features a sketch of the part, and users indicate on it where the defect appeared on the part. Figure 3.6 shows an example of a check sheet for location.

Figure 3.6
Location check sheet

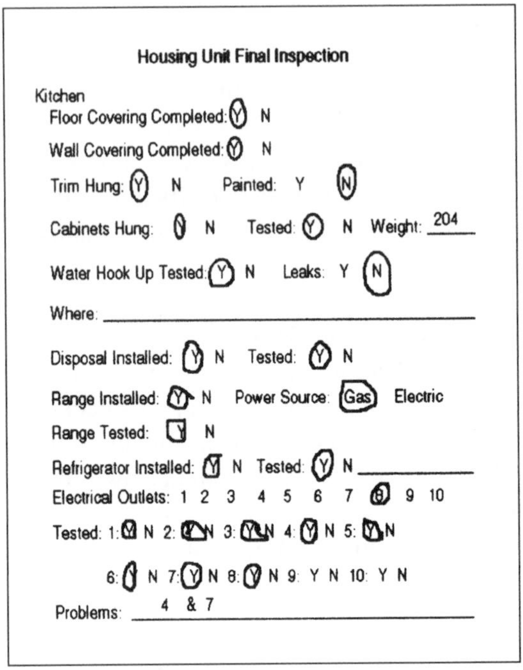

Housing Unit Final Inspection

Kitchen
Floor Covering Completed: (Y) N
Wall Covering Completed: (Y) N
Trim Hung: (Y) N   Painted: Y (N)
Cabinets Hung: (Y) N   Tested: (Y) N Weight: _204_
Water Hook Up Tested: (Y) N   Leaks: Y (N)
Where: _____
Disposal Installed: (Y) N   Tested: (Y) N
Range Installed: (Y) N   Power Source (Gas) Electric
Range Tested: (Y) N
Refrigerator Installed: (Y) N Tested: (Y) N _____
Electrical Outlets: 1 2 3   4 5 6   7 (8) 9 10
Tested: 1: (Y) N 2: (Y)N 3: (Y)N 4: (Y) N 5: (Y)N
      6: (Y) N 7: (Y) N 8: (Y) N 9: Y N 10: Y N
Problems: _____ 4 & 7 _____

Figure 3.7
Final inspection check
sheet

Check Sheets for Final Inspection

Check sheets for final inspection are used to verify if all final quality checks have been made. These check sheets usually list product features and include a place to mark if the product passed or failed the inspection at that point. Sometimes called *traveling check sheets*, these go with the product at each stage of the final testing. Figure 3.7 shows a sample check sheet for final inspection.

A final note about check sheets: Both the accuracy and the consistency of the data depend on each user's interpretation of defects and how to record them. To ensure both, users should receive standardized training on what to look for, what to record, and how to record it, etc.

As mentioned in Chapter 1, everyone the solution might affect should be a part of the solution process. This ensures that the impact on each department is considered in the final solution. Involving everyone also gives you more options, since each person will have his or her own perspective on the problem.

4.0 Problem-solving techniques

...when you have eliminated the impossible, whatever
remains, however improbable, must be the truth.
Sherlock Holmes

The first step toward solving a problem is defining it. This makes
the objective clear for everyone involved so they can focus on
finding a solution. It also lets you tackle the problem head-on
instead of being sidetracked with its symptoms.

Obviously, you can't solve a problem if you don't know what's
causing it. So, the second step toward solving a problem is to
determine its cause or causes.

Once you have defined a problem and found its causes, you can
work on correcting it. It's important to consider the solution's
impact on other parts of the process before you adopt it. Equally
important is how to prevent the problem from happening again. This
is the idea behind SPC: preventing problems instead of detecting
and solving them.

There are several tools that make problems easier to define and
solve. This chapter looks at some of these and describes how to use
them.

4.1 Pareto analysis

Sometimes the hardest part of solving problems is deciding which
one to tackle first. Pareto analysis helps you decide. Pareto is a way
to prioritize problems by looking at their cost and frequency. It also
helps you determine which causes are the biggest.

Vilfredo Pareto, a 19th Century economist, developed this technique
while studying the distribution of wealth in society. In his study, he
found that just a few people control the largest share of the wealth,

with the majority of the people controlling the small amount left. It is this idea of "the vital few and the trivial many" that Pareto analysis is based on.

The idea of "the vital few and the trivial many" applies to industrial problems as well as it does to economics. Normally, a few production problems cause the most damage and a large number of problems do the rest. The goal of Pareto analysis is to clearly identify which problems could represent the largest potential savings.

Project team members use Pareto to analyze problems and develop a schedule for attacking them. They also use it to show how the process has improved over time.

Pareto breaks problems into a series of categories, with a common denominator running through each. In most cases this denominator is dollars, since most problems reflect added costs for a company. However, if costs are about the same for each problem area, you may want to focus on how often each problem occurs.

The result of Pareto is a combination bar chart and line plot showing which causes occur most often and at what cost. Figure 4.1 shows the data collected for a Pareto chart. Figure 4.2 shows the Pareto chart produced from this data.

Date: 4/17/02		Number Inspected: 723		
Item	Cost	# Defects	% Defects	Total Cost
Air conditioning	$250.75	127	10.96	$31,845.25
Back flasher	112.00	203	17.53	22,736.00
Front flasher	112.00	115	9.93	12,880.00
Hazard lights	83.50	92	7.95	8,602.00
Power locks	143.00	57	4.92	8,151.00
Power mirrors	157.75	45	3.89	7,098.75
Fr. turn signal	53.00	126	10.89	6,678.00
Tailgate	300.00	22	1.90	6,600.00
Defogger	78.95	81	7.00	6,394.95
Power brakes	325.00	18	1.56	5,850.00
Stereo	200.00	24	2.07	4,800.00
Power seats	75.00	61	5.27	4,575.00
Other	102.73	187	16.13	19,210.51
Total		1,158	100	$145,421.46

Figure 4.1
Data for Pareto analysis

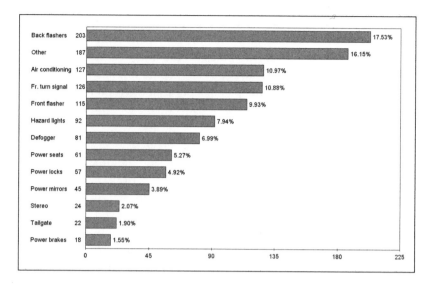

Figure 4.2
Pareto chart

To set up a Pareto chart:

Step 1: Set up categories
The first step in setting up Pareto analysis is to define the categories. Categories should correspond with potential areas of action, such a defect type, machine or department. Grouping by cost or correction time won't provide the proper focus. Operators, since they are closest to process problems, will likely have a good idea of how to group the data. In Figure 4.1, the defect type is used to define the categories.

Six to ten categories are usually enough for Pareto analysis. Too few categories probably won't break the problem into small enough "bites" to be effective, and too many categories make the study too broad. After identifying the major categories, lump the remaining problems into an "other" category. "Other" may contain several categories, some of which may be broken out for detailed analysis after today's major problems have been reduced to one of the trivial ones.

Step 2: Determine the time frame
After determining the categories, set the time period for your analysis. Problems occur at varying times, so the time you select should allow the less frequent ones to occur but should not postpone action or go too far into past records. You should set the time frame before the analysis begins.

Step 3: Collect the data
Record how frequently a problem occurs during the time period. Figures 4.1 and 4.2 use data from a two-week period.

Step 4: Summarize data in tabular form
Set up a table with columns for the category name, how often it occurred, the estimated cost per defect for each category, and the total cost for each category.

Enter the category names in the table. Next, enter the number of times each category occurred during the study period.

Now, enter the estimated average cost per defect. This figure should include indirect costs such as extra handling, storage space, paperwork, shipping and new packaging. The cost per defect can be an estimate. As long as it is relative to each of the various categories, the exact cost is not critical.

Finally, multiply how often the problem occurred by the cost per defect, and enter this figure in the total cost for each category.

Step 5: Create the chart
Draw a horizontal and a vertical axis. Divide one axis into segments for each category, including "other." The other axis should be divided into segments based on the common denominator, in this case, dollars.

Sort the categories by your common denominator, and draw a bar for each on the chart in this order. Begin with the most costly problem and end with "other," even if other is greater. The length or height of the bar should correspond to the denominator value.

An SPC software program can make this whole process easy, by calculating and drawing the graphics for you.

Finally, when using Pareto to decide how to tackle your problems, keep in mind that it is usually easier to reduce the most frequent problem than it is to totally eliminate a less common one. And it will most likely show more immediate savings.

4.2 Brainstorming

Brainstorming is a proven technique for solving problems. It is a rapid-fire method of coming up with possible solutions without lingering on any of them. Although individuals can use this technique, it is more effective when used by a group. Groups are more effective because one person's idea can ignite ideas from other group members.

There are five rules for brainstorming:

1. Set a time limit.
For most problems, a limit of 15 minutes to an hour will be adequate.

2. Identify the specific target.
The topic does not have to be a problem. Brainstorming can help identify solutions, possible causes, inputs or outputs. Select and display the topic before the session begins.

3. Generate as many ideas as possible within the time limit.
The goal of brainstorming is to create as many ideas as possible. Include any twist to an old idea, as well as any "off the wall" ideas.

4. Appoint one person as recorder.
Brainstorming is most effective when the ideas are written for the group to see during the session. A blackboard or flip chart sheets hung from walls are good ways to record ideas. They make it easier for members to recall previous ideas, and to spin new ideas off old ones. All ideas should be recorded, even the silly ones and the minor changes to old ones.

5. *Avoid evaluation, criticism and all forms of judgment, good or bad, until the session is over.*

Whether ideas are practical or not will be decided later. Silly ideas can open new channels of thought, which can lead to a more practical solution, so they should be encouraged.

Criticism, even a snicker, can discourage people from offering their ideas and will limit the group's potential. This can also happen if one or two people control the session with their ideas. You can avoid this by going around the group and asking each member for an idea. Although everyone may not have an idea in every go-around, with an equal chance to participate, the group will come up with more ideas.

If you want to generate additional ideas, give group members a copy of all the ideas from the brainstorming session so they can add any new ideas they come up with. Then arrange a wrap-up session for members to present any new ideas, or come up with other ones. The period between the initial session and the wrap-up can be days or weeks depending on how critical the problem is.

If the problem is critical, or when you feel there are enough suggestions, it is time to evaluate the merits and feasibility of each idea. Set up criteria for accepting or rejecting an idea, and run through the list discarding those that don't meet the group's requirements. After narrowing down the list to a few ideas, the group can decide which course of action to take.

Another diagramming tool that helps a team organize a large amount of brainstorming information is the *affinity diagram*. Affinity diagrams group together ideas that have common characteristics. Post-it® Notes or index cards are often helpful in organizing these ideas into meaningful categories.

4.3 Cause and effect diagrams

After a problem is defined, its causes must be determined. Cause and effect diagrams, also known as Ishikawa or fishbone diagrams, show how to sort out and relate factors affecting quality. By illustrating how each cause relates to the effect, this diagram guides problem-solving efforts to the disease, not the symptom.

Cause-and-effect diagrams break the causes into several categories and then subdivide these further when they become too complex. Most major causes can be categorized as:

- Materials
- Equipment
- Workers
- Methods
- Measurement
- Management
- Environment

There are four steps in drawing a cause-and effect diagram:

1. Determine what characteristic you want to improve and control.

2. Write this "effect" down.
Put the effect in a box on the right side of the page and draw a broad arrow from the left of the page to this box. An example of this appears in Figure 4.4.

Figure 4.4
The second step in cause-and-effect diagramming

3. Write the major categories along the top and bottom of the arrow.
Allow space between the categories and between the category and the arrow. Then box off the categories, and draw an arrow from each to the main arrow. Figure 4.5 shows an example of this step.

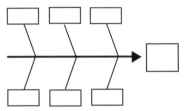

Figure 4.5
The third step in cause-and-
effect diagramming

4. List the factors that may be the causes as branches for each category.

If one cause can affect more than one category, list it for each. Any factors that might contribute to a cause should branch out from that cause, as shown in Figure 4.6.

As with brainstorming, a group approach is the most effective way to create a cause-and-effect diagram. The goal is to identify all of the causes that relate to the effect, and groups usually come up with more ideas than individuals do.

After completing the diagram, the group should identify which factors in each area have the most impact on the effect under study. Any attempt to improve the effect will probably address one of these factors.

4.4 Scatter diagrams

Scatter diagrams show if there is a relationship between a cause and the effects, or between two causes. They can reveal if an increase in one variable increases, decreases, or has no effect on the other one.

To draw a scatter diagram:

1. Collect pairs of data for the variables in the study.

2. Draw vertical and horizontal axes.
Axes should be roughly the same length. Add tick marks to represent the type of data for each variable on its respective axis, as shown in Figure 4.7A.

3. Plot the pairs of data on the graph.
For repeated values, make concentric circles around the original point.

If there is a relationship between the variables, the plots will form a cigar shape. The stronger the relationship, the tighter this shape will be. The shape of the points shows the type of correlation as shown in Figure 4.7B - 4.7D.

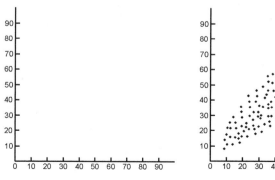
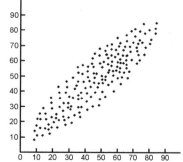

Figure 4.7A
Setup for a scatter diagram

Figure 4.7B
Positive correlation

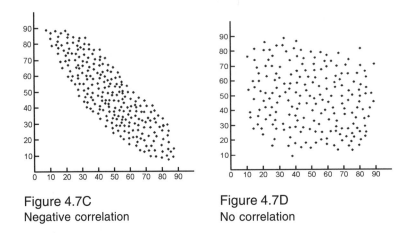

Figure 4.7C
Negative correlation

Figure 4.7D
No correlation

Figure 4.7B shows a positive correlation. In this case, increasing the cause increased the effect.

Figure 4.7C shows a negative correlation; increasing the cause decreased the effect.

Figure 4.7D shows no correlation between the two variables.

4.5 Histograms

Histograms illustrate how often a range of measurements has occurred. They also show how the data distribution relates to the specs and if data falls outside the spec limits. By showing the shape, central value, and the method of dispersion of a group of measurements, histograms can tell us a lot about the behavior of a process.

To set up a histogram:

1. Collect and record data.
For more information on the type of data to collect and ways to record it, see Chapter 3.

2. Determine the minimum and maximum values of the data.
Look for the largest and smallest values.

3. Determine the number of groups or cells needed.
A good rule of thumb is to have the number of groups roughly equal to the square root of the number of observations.

4. Decide the range of values for each group.
This range must be the same size for all groups, and is easier to work with if the values are rounded off. You may want to make the ranges begin and end with a value that falls halfway between two data values, so there is no question where the data should fall.

5. Set the width for the cells.
This is done by dividing the range of the data (maximum-minimum) by the number of cells.

Part No. _453568_ Date: _5/18/92_ Operator: _Frank T._

Machine: _127_ Shift: _2_ Supervisor: _JFM_

Class	Range	Count	Total Count
1	0.995 - 1.895	/////	5
2	1.895 - 2.785	///////	7
3	2.785 - 3.675	////////	8
4	3.675 - 4.565	//////////	10
5	4.565 - 5.445	/////////////	13
6	5.445 - 6.335	//////////	10
7	6.335 - 7.225	////////	8
8	7.225 - 8.115	able//////	6
9	8.115 - 9.005	////	4
	Total Readings:		71

6. Draw a table to tally the data.
Each row in the table should reflect a range for the histogram.

7. Tally the data.
Go through the data and put a mark in the appropriate row for each data point. Then total up the number of marks for each row, as shown in Figure 4.8.

Figure 4.8
Tally or check sheet for creating a histogram

8. Draw the horizontal and vertical axes.
Both should be long enough to include all data points. You may also want to draw a line for the production target and the upper and lower spec limits on the histogram.

9. Draw the bars on the chart.
We determined the width of each bar in Step 5. The height of each should equal the frequency recorded in the table. Figure 4.9A shows a complete histogram, drawn from the data tallied above.

How you interpret the chart depends on your objective and the data distribution. A near normal shape usually means process variation comes from common causes. A normal distribution is symmetrical, as shown in Figure 4.9B. This is described further in Chapter 2.

How close the actual distribution is to a normal curve can tell a lot about a process. Although we can often see if distribution is close to normal, we can't always identify the subtle shifts that represent a process problem. This is especially true when we try to compare histograms.

To address this, statisticians have developed several methods for testing the data for normality. Among these are tests for skewness and kurtosis, and Chi-square tests. With these tests, we can detect differences in data distributions that have the same mean and the same standard deviation. This type of analysis can show us if process improvements are effective.

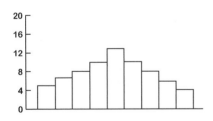

Figure 4.9A
Histogram from the data shown
in Figure 4.8

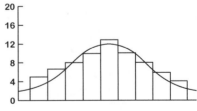

Figure 4.9B
Histogram with curve showing
a normal distribution

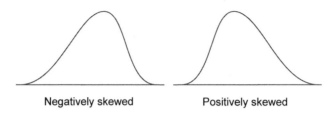

Negatively skewed   Positively skewed

Figure 4.10
Illustration of positive and negative skew

Skew is the difference between the mean and the mode. Tests for
skewness measure the symmetry of the curve. If the skew
factor is zero, there is no skew. If the skew factor is positive, the
mean is larger than the mode. With a negative skew, the mode is
larger than the mean. Figure 4.10 shows curves with positive and
negative skew.

The formula for determining the skew factor is:

$$\frac{\Sigma\,(y - \mu)^3}{\sigma^4}$$

Where y = the deviation, m = the mean, and σ = the standard deviation.

Along with letting you compare histograms, the skew factor can tell
you if the process has a tendency to lean toward upper or lower
specification limits.

There are also situations where the standard deviation, the mean,
and the skew are the same for two distributions, but one chart has a
flat curve and the other a peaked curve. The degree of flatness of
the curve is known as the *kurtosis*.

The following formula is used to determine the degree of kurtosis:

$$\frac{\Sigma\,(y - \mu)^3}{\sigma^4} - 3$$

Where y = the deviation, μ = the mean, and σ = the standard deviation.

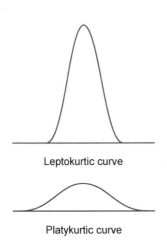

Leptokurtic curve

Platykurtic curve

Figure 4.11
Illustration of Leptokurtic
and Platykurtic curves

If the result of this formula equals zero, the curve is normal. If it is greater than zero, the curve is flatter than the normal curve or *platykurtic*. If it is less than zero, the curve is higher than the normal curve, or *leptokurtic*. Figure 4.11 shows platykurtic and leptokurtic curves.

The Chi-square test shows how well the actual distribution fits the expected one. These tests are often used to determine the likelihood of a distribution.

Most statistical software programs can compute the Chi-square value.

The formula for Chi-square (χ^2) is:

$$\chi^2 = \Sigma \frac{(f_a - f_e)}{f_e}$$

Where f_a = the actual frequency and f_e = the estimated or previous frequency.

The resulting value must be compared to the Chi-square table (Appendix B) to determine its significance.

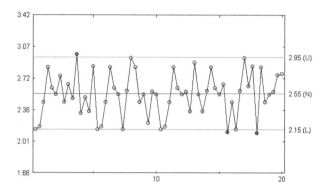

Figure 4.12
Run chart

4.6 Run charts

Run charts provide a way to study the stability of a process and to detect process trends. Because they reflect the process over time, data is plotted on the chart in the order that it was produced.

The X-axis of a run chart is usually a simple count of the data, with the first entry being 1, the second 2, and so on. The Y-axis shows the value of the data. Figure 4.12 shows a run chart.

5.0 General concepts of control charting

To improve is to change;
to be perfect is to change often.

Winston Churchill

Control charts provide us with a picture of our process that can be easily understood. They are a way to map the process, showing us when and where variability occurs so we can evaluate and adjust the process and monitor the results of our adjustments. They allow us to see even subtle shifts in the process that we might miss if we just looked at lists of data.

5.1 The meaning of limits

You've heard the quote "nobody notices when things go right." We do notice when things go wrong and have learned to respond when they do. This is why SPC leads to improvement. Have you ever heard of a Compliments Desk in a store? Probably not. That's because we expect everything to go right and consider "right" to be the normal state of affairs.

Statistics show us just how good and how bad a process or output can be and still be "normal." How we define normal, in this case, must be based on the actual history of the operation. If we ask someone to define how the operation should work, they will most likely describe a perfect operation. However, for an accurate picture of the actual situation we need to ask how they expect the process to behave.

It is easy to predict the operations level with historical data. If we measure "enough" parts, we can calculate how much they "typically" vary from the target. This typical value, the average, is our prediction for how close future parts will be to their target. Remember, we can't predict the behavior of the individual parts, but we can predict the distribution for a group.

In Chapter 1, we looked at variability and how we can't expect any group of parts to hit our predicted target exactly. Because of this, we develop estimates of how far the parts can be from the prediction and still have variance caused by sampling rather than changes in the process. Each sample will have a different average value, but it will be within these limits.

For example, let's say I give you a deck of cards. I tell you that I may have substituted red cards for none, some, or all of the black cards in the deck. You have no idea how many red cards are in the deck.

If you draw one card and it is red, you have sampled with n = 1. Your statistic, the count of red cards, implies a distribution of 100% red in the deck. If a fair deck is 50% red, how much would you be willing to bet that this is not a fair deck?

You draw another card. It, too, is red. Now how much would you want to bet the deck is fair? You have more information, but it still is not quite enough. You draw 20 cards and all of them are red. Do think the deck is half red? Probably not. The odds of drawing 20 out of 20 red cards from a fair deck are so small there is not much risk in saying the deck is not fair.

With 20 cards, you can see that the odds are more than enough to make a safe bet. You could, however, make a safe bet with fewer cards. If you want to be correct 996 times out of 1,000, how many red cards must you draw without any black cards appearing?

The answer is eight. If eight cards of one color appear, there are less than four chances in 1,000 that the deck is fair. We have just developed control limits for betting the deck has not changed with the risk of error being roughly 0.4%.

Now suppose I hand you a series of card decks. You draw 20 cards from each and plot the number of red cards. If there are less than

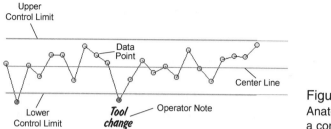

Figure 5.1
Anatomy of
a control chart

eight red or more than zero red, you call the deck fair. If the count exceeds either limit, you'll say the deck was changed.

Now let's see how the plot is drawn. Figure 5.1 shows a portion of a control chart. The center line is our average value, or prediction for the most likely outcome. The upper control limit is the highest number of red cards we can count and say nothing has changed. The lower control limit is the lowest number of red cards we can count and still say the process hasn't changed. We plot the actual counts on this chart.

To take this idea a step further, let's call the red cards bad and the black ones good. If we sample a series of decks and see no sign that they are unfair, we won't change the process. If we start to produce decks with more red cards, we should stop the process and find out why we are getting too many red cards. Once we know the cause of the unfair decks, we can change the system to prevent this cause from recurring.

Now suppose we find eight black cards in a sample from our process. We conclude our process has changed so that we now produce more black cards than we did when we set up the limits. In this case, we would again stop the process to find the cause of the increase in black cards. Since, for this example, it's better to have more than 50% black cards, we would want to change the process so it consistently produces decks that are more than 50% black.

Once we change the system of producing card decks, our old rules for testing the decks are outdated. We must recalculate the new average number of red cards in the decks. Then we need to create new limits for how many red we will allow before we say the process has changed to a new level.

Sample averages or ranges reflect any change in the population and give us a statistical signal similar to getting eight cards of one color. This signal only tells us that something has changed, not why it changed. We have to use our engineering and operating knowledge to find the cause or causes and act on them.

If there aren't any statistical signals from the process, we say the process is in a state of statistical control. This means there are no signs of change in the process. It doesn't mean we are happy with it, just that it is stable and unchanging.

If a change is signaled, and we have evidence that the process has changed, we say the process is "out of control." Out-of-control in the statistical sense can be a good thing. If the process is never out of statistical control, there will never be a reason to make changes in it, and your quality and productivity won't change. If we remove the causes of undesirable changes and maintain the causes of good ones, our quality, productivity, and costs will improve.

Statistical control is the first step toward achieving the desired operating level. After all, if you can't ask an operator to make exactly 15% bad parts every day, how can you ask him or her to make exactly 0% or even 1%?

5.2 Two modes of change in a process: average & dispersion

With the mean and standard deviation, we can completely describe the normal curve. To track the process behavior of variable data, we must monitor both parameters.

We can detect a shift in the process average by a change in the behavior of the sample averages. Likewise, when we watch the action of one measure of spread, we can detect changes in the spread of our process. We use a chart of sample averages, or X-

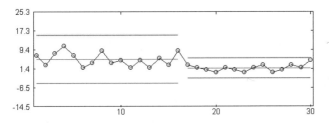

Figure 5.2
X-bar chart showing fewer red cards (a shift in the process)

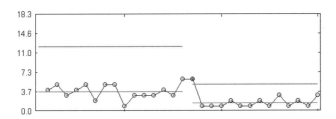

Figure 5.3
R chart showing a shift toward less variance within the
number of red cards drawn within each sample

bars to look for changes in the process average. We take readings
for a sample, and plot their average. Any unusual activity in these
averages shows changes in the average value for the process. Figure
5.2 shows an X-bar chart of our card samples.

Plotting the range is the most common way to monitor for changes
in the process dispersion. We plot the the difference between high
and low readings for a sample. Abnormal behavior in these samples
points to changes in the process variability. Figure 5.3 shows a
range chart of our card samples.

5.3 Prediction: the key to timely detection of changes

If our study shows an out of control condition, we can detect when
the process or parts differ from our prediction. The key to detecting
these changes quickly is the ability to predict. If we monitor the

process, but don't report what has occurred until the end of the month, we would simply have historical information. There would be no way to change the process operations for that month.

However, if we predict the level and variability we expect to see in a process, we can compare the process to this prediction regularly. As soon as we find a deviation from the prediction, we can begin to make corrections.

How do we make our predictions with enough confidence that we can act when a change is signaled? In Chapter 2, we discussed using the average deviation from the target value to predict the normal error in parts. We said that with "enough" samples averaged together we could have confidence in our expected value. How many samples are enough?

Twenty to 25 samples are enough for most purposes. After collecting the samples, calculate their averages and ranges, and control limits. These control limits will apply to this data. If there aren't signs of out-of-control behavior, we have enough proof that our prediction about the next sample group is as accurate as we can expect it to be.

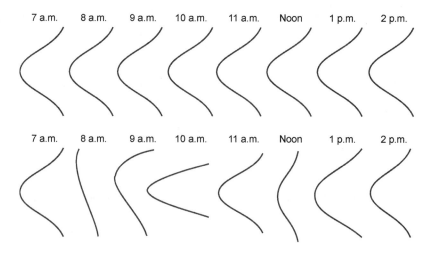

Figure 5.4
Stable and unstable processes

If you look at Figure 5.4, you'll see the upper diagram shows a stable process. A stable process is one that has very similar distributions over time. With this pattern, we have no problem predicting the shape of the distribution for the next sample. If the process is unstable, as shown in the lower diagram, we are unable to make any prediction about the next sample.

5.4 Variation within and between samples

With variable data, we can use the variability between each reading within a sample to make predictions and the variability between samples to find problems.

The variability between each reading gives us a better idea of how much the sample averages will vary than if we just looked at the sample averages. This extra evidence provides us with a more complete picture of process variability.

In the section on sampling in Chapter 3, we talked about taking readings for a sample from consecutive parts. When we do this, we create a "snapshot" of that time in the process. If we compare these snapshots we can determine if the variation is a normal part of the process or not. Variation we find between these snapshots has a special cause, and we'll want to remove it from our production process.

As we design our control system, this information helps us determine which sources of variation are a normal part of our process, and which are not. For example, suppose your process has two machines run by one person. If you consider the variability between the machines to be part of the process, include readings from both machines in each sample. If you think the variability is behaving differently, each sample should have readings from one machine or the other. This will tell you if there is more variability from the two machines than you predicted for one machine.

5.5 Trial limits, control limits and recalculation points

When you begin a control chart, there is no way to be sure the original data didn't have any special cause variation. Because of this, we consider the first set of control limits to be trial limits. We test trial limits for a time to see if they actually are right for our process.

For some of our tests we'll find the trial data shows a lack of control, but by the time we finish testing the limits we've lost the ability to trace the problem. Throwing out the trial data would change our predictions of what to expect in the future. We must therefore keep the data as a historical record of the process.

We use statistics to describe, without bias, what we expect the process to produce. We base these expectations on historical information. There will be times that the process changes so the conditions under which the limits were calculated no longer exist. When this happens we can't use the same limits to make predictions and should set new ones. If the change was not deliberate, we need to make sure the process really is different before we set new limits.

5.6 The concept of continuous improvement

It's hard to tell if our process is getting better when we only measure bad parts. If we measure both good and bad parts, control charts give us a statistical signal when any change occurs in the process. Whenever the charts signal a process change, the person responsible for the process must decide if the change was good or bad. Control charts make it possible to notice when things go right as well as wrong.

By now you recognize that the more we reduce process variability the more sure we can be of our predictions. Reducing variability also makes it easier to detect smaller changes in the process. If we react to these, we have better control of the output and a better product. The level of product quality will also be more consistent.

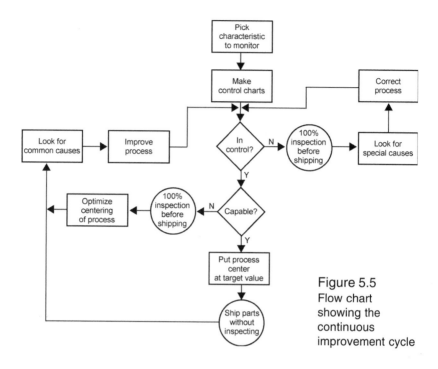

Figure 5.5
Flow chart
showing the
continuous
improvement cycle

When you reduce the variability and center the process around a target value, there is a greater chance that the customer will receive a product that's on target. As the product improves, customer satisfaction increases, which then increases business, etc.

We can set our statistical trap for process changes and sit by waiting to see what falls in. Or we can try to improve the process without prompting. Once we define how the process behaves we won't worry so much about making changes that might upset the apple cart. With quick feedback to signal good and bad results, we can try new ideas, and immediately reverse any that don't work.

Continuous improvement is a never ending cycle of process improvement as shown in Figure 5.5. We must continue to improve our process to improve our product and remain competitive.

6.0 Control charts for variable data

*Quality is never an accident; it is always
the result of intelligent effort.*

John Ruskin

6.1 X-bar & R charts

In the last chapter we looked at concepts of control charting. In this
chapter we'll look at how to create control charts for variable data.

As discussed in Chapter 3, variable data comes from measurements
such as length, weight, depth, diameter, temperature, or time.
Variable data can be whole numbers or fractions. This type of data
reveals a lot of information with just a few readings. It not only
shows if a reading is too big or too small, but also shows by *how
much*.

The X-bar & R charts, described in Chapter 5, are the most common
charts used for studying variable data.

To create X-bar & R charts:

1. Collect and record the data.
Include the date, the operation or process involved, the sample size,
and how often samples are taken. Chapter 3 has more information
on collecting and recording data, and on creating check sheets.
Although you can draw a control chart on graph paper, you may
want to create a form that shows the data or a summary of each
sample as well as the charts. If you design a form, leave a space for
notes which should be written directly on the chart for quick reference. A sample of this type of form is shown in Figure 6.1. The
back of this sample has a worksheet area for calculating the limits.

If you want to know when variation occurs, you must record and
then plot data in the order you collected it.

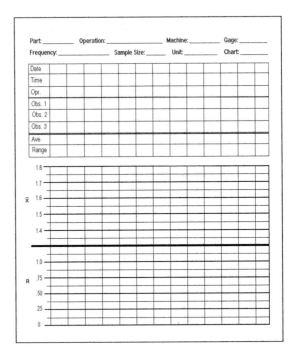

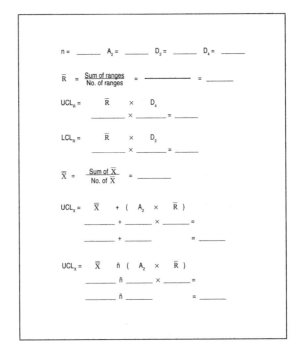

Figure 6.1
X-bar & R chart form

2. Draw two charts, one for average data and one for range data. Draw a separate Y axis for each chart, so that the scales can differ. The X-axis is the same for both charts.

Step 3: Calculate average and range for each sample.
To calculate the *sample average* or X-bar, add the readings in the sample together and divide this total by the number of readings. For example:

$$1.56 + 1.47 + 1.62 + 1.42 = 6.07$$

$$6.07 / 4 = 1.52$$

To calculate the *sample range***,** find the sample's largest and smallest readings. Subtract the smallest reading from the largest. Remember, if a value is negative, it becomes a positive value when subtracted. For example:

$$1.62 - 1.42 = 0.20 \text{ or } 1.62 - (-1.42) = 3.04.$$

Figure 6.2 shows a form with the readings taken, average and range calculated, and the data plotted.

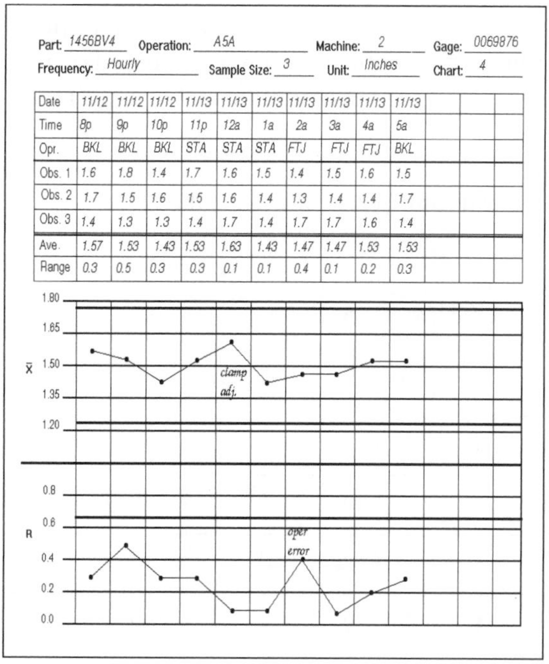

Part: 1456BV4 Operation: A5A Machine: 2 Gage: 0069876
Frequency: Hourly Sample Size: 3 Unit: Inches Chart: 4

Date	11/12	11/12	11/12	11/13	11/13	11/13	11/13	11/13	11/13	11/13			
Time	8p	9p	10p	11p	12a	1a	2a	3a	4a	5a			
Opr.	BKL	BKL	BKL	STA	STA	STA	FTJ	FTJ	FTJ	BKL			
Obs. 1	1.6	1.8	1.4	1.7	1.6	1.5	1.4	1.5	1.6	1.5			
Obs. 2	1.7	1.5	1.6	1.5	1.6	1.4	1.3	1.4	1.4	1.7			
Obs. 3	1.4	1.3	1.3	1.4	1.7	1.4	1.7	1.7	1.6	1.4			
Ave.	1.57	1.53	1.43	1.53	1.63	1.43	1.47	1.47	1.53	1.53			
Range	0.3	0.5	0.3	0.3	0.1	0.1	0.4	0.1	0.2	0.3			

Figure 6.2
X-bar & R chart

4. Calculate trial control limits for the range chart.

Calculate trial limits from the first 20 to 25 samples. Then, compare to these to your sample values to determine statistical control. Although it is possible to set control limits with fewer samples, it is better to use at least 20. Control limits based on fewer samples are often less reliable.

4a. To calculate the limits for the range chart, we must first calculate the average range.

We do this by adding all the range values together and dividing this total by the number of samples. For example:

$$0.02 + 0.05 + 1.0 + 0.04 + 0.08 = 1.19$$

$$1.19 / 5 = 0.24$$

The average range is symbolized as R-bar ($\overline{R}$), and it forms the center line (C_R) of the range chart.

4b. After finding the average of the range, calculate the upper and lower control limits.

The formulas used for control limits include a factor that simplifies the calculations. These factors, as Table 6.1 shows, are based on the size of the sample n. (An expanded version of this table appears in Appendix C).

For the range's upper control limit (UCL_R), we use the D_4 factor. The UCL_R formula is:

$$UCL_R = D_4 * \overline{R}$$

n	A_2	D_3	D_4	d_2
2	1.880	—	3.267	1.128
3	1.023	—	2.575	1.693
4	0.729	—	2.282	2.059

Table 6.1
Control limits factors

Sample \ Obs.	1	2	3	4	5	6	7	8	9	10
1	2.15	2.84	2.74	2.49	2.50	2.15	2.84	2.15	2.84	2.22
2	2.18	2.61	2.45	2.98	2.35	2.18	2.61	2.58	2.45	2.57
3	2.45	2.54	2.65	2.33	2.85	2.45	2.54	2.94	2.54	2.54
Range	0.3	0.3	0.29	0.65	0.5	0.3	0.3	0.79	0.39	0.35

Sample \ Obs.	11	12	13	14	15	16	17	18	19	20
1	2.15	2.84	2.57	2.54	2.84	2.65	2.15	2.63	2.84	2.57
2	2.18	2.61	2.35	2.35	2.61	2.12	2.58	2.85	2.45	2.75
3	2.45	2.54	2.89	2.58	2.54	2.45	2.94	2.11	2.54	2.77
Range	0.3	0.3	0.54	0.23	0.3	0.53	0.79	0.74	0.39	0.2

Table 6.2

For example, a chart with the sample size of three, and ranges values of 0.27, 0.54, 0.89, 0.31, 0.63, 0.98, and 0.12 would have an average range of 0.53. The UCL_R would be 2.575 $*$ 0.53 or 1.364.

The lower control limit (LCL_R) uses the D_3 factor for which there is no value if the sample size is six or less. In these cases the LCL_R is always zero, since range can't be less than zero.

The formula for LCL_R is:

$$LCL_R = D_3 * \overline{R}$$

For example, using the data from the example above, we find the $LCL_R = 0$.

Or, if we base our limits on the 20 samples shown in Table 6.2:

The $\overline{R}$ for these samples $= 0.3 + 0.3 + 0.29 + 0.65 + 0.5 + 0.3 + 0.3 + 0.79 + 0.39 + 0.35 + 0.3 + 0.3 + 0.54 + 0.23 + 0.3 + 0.53 + 0.79 + 0.74 + 0.39 + 0.2 = 8.49 / 20 = 0.4245$.

The $UCL_R = D_4 \times \overline{R} = 2.575 * 0.4245 = 1.093$, and the $LCL_R = D_3 * \overline{R} = 0 * 0.4245 = 0.00$.

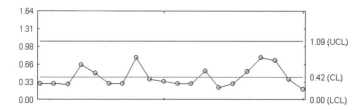

Figure 6.3
R-chart created from our 20 samples.

Figure 6.3 shows an R-chart of this data.

5. We need to set the chart's scale before we draw the control limits on the R-chart.
A good rule of thumb is to set a scale for the R-chart so the upper control limit is about two-thirds of the height of the chart. Keep in mind this is only an approximate scale and you may need to adjust it to accommodate some data. One way to estimate scale is by dividing the UCL_R by 2 and adding that value to the UCL or subtracting it from the LCL. For example:

$$1.093 / 2 = 0.5465 + 1.093 = 1.6395$$

The minimum scale value for range can't be less than zero.

6. Draw the control limits and plot the range points on the range chart.
If any points are out of control, check the data to see if they are reasonable and check the calculations for accuracy.

7. Trial control limits for the X-bar chart.
We use the R-bar value to calculate these limits, so it's a good idea to confirm this value before moving to the X-bar chart.

7a. The center line value is the average of the sample averages.
We find this by adding all the sample averages together and dividing this total by the number of samples. For example:

$$1.57 + 1.62 + 1.38 + 1.74 = 6.31 / 4 = 1.578$$

This value is called an Xdouble-bar and is symbolized as $\overline{\overline{X}}$.

7b. Find the upper control limit for the X-bar chart.
We use the A_2 factor from the table of factors and the R-bar value to find the upper control limit for the X-bar chart (UCL_x). The UCL_x formula is:

$$UCL_x = \overline{\overline{X}} + (A_2 * \overline{R})$$

For example, a chart with the sample size of three, an R-bar of 0.53, and X-bar value of 1.25, 1.34, 1.11, 1.48, and 1.02 would have a Xdouble-bar of 1.24. The UCL_X would be:

$$(1.023 * 0.53) + 1.24 = 0.542 + 1.24 = 1.782$$

7c. Find the X-bar chart's lower control limit.
For the X-bar chart's lower control limit (LCL_x) we again use the A_2 factor. This formula is:

$$LCL_X = \overline{\overline{X}} - (A_2 * \overline{R})$$

If we use the data from the example above, the LCL_X is:

$$1.24 - (1.023 * 0.53) = 1.24 - 0.542 = 0.698$$

8. Before we draw the control limits on the X-bar chart, we need to set its scale.
In this case we try to make the area within the upper and lower limits about one half of the total chart. One way to estimate the scale for the X-bar chart is to subtract the lower control limit from the upper control limit and divide this value by two. For the maximum scale, add this value to the UCL_X. For the minimum scale, subtract this value from the LCL_X. For example if the UCL_X is 2.967 and the LCL_X is 2.082, you calculate the scale as:

$$2.967 - 2.082 = 0.885 / 2 = 0.4425$$
$$2.967 + 0.4425 = 3.4095 \text{ (maximum scale value)}$$
$$2.082 - 0.4425 = 1.6395 \text{ (minimum scale value)}$$

Obs.	1	2	3	4	5	6	7	8	9	10
Avg.	2.26	2.663	2.613	2.6	2.567	2.26	2.663	2.557	2.61	2.443

Obs.	11	12	13	14	15	16	17	18	19	20
Avg.	2.26	2.663	2.603	2.49	2.663	2.407	2.557	2.53	2.61	2.697

Table 6.3

If we use the 20 samples from Table 6.2 for our X-bar chart, we would have the sample averages shown in Table 6.3.

The Xdouble bar is 2.536. The upper control limit is:

$$2.536 + (1.023 * 0.4245) = 2.536 + 0.4343 = 2.9703$$

The lower control limit is:

$$2.536 - 0.4343 = 2.102$$

The scale would be 3.404 – 1.668. Figure 6.3 shows an X-bar chart of this data.

9. Draw control limits and plot sample averages on the X-bar chart.
Again, if any points fall outside the control limits, check the data and calculations.

We base our predictions of how a process will behave in the future on how it behaved in the past. Control limits show us the past operating range, and we extend them to show the course we predict the

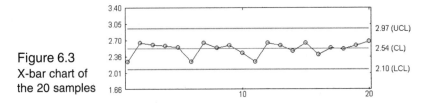

Figure 6.3
X-bar chart of
the 20 samples

process will take. When designing a control chart, draw the control limits well past the samples you've based them on. It is also a good idea to vary or highlight the lines so you can easily tell the difference between the calculated and projected control limits.

Extending the limits for future data before we plot new data allows us to compare the current process conditions to those of the past. Since limits are a prediction of the process, a point that falls outside the limit on either chart tells us there is a change in the process.

Investigate any points that fall outside the limits as they may indicate a problem. If there is a problem, you'll want find the cause, take steps to correct it and to prevent its recurrence. You also will want to find the cause of change that improve the process, so you can make them a part of normal process operations.

Calculate new control limits only when there is a change in the process as shown by samples that fall out of the control limits. Calculating control limits without a change in the process leads to 'floating' limits. Floating limits change gradually over time, but don't signal a change in the process. Figure 6.4A shows an X-bar chart with floating control limits. Figure 6.4B shows an X-bar chart with control limits that shifted after the process changed.

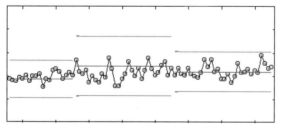

Figure 6.4A
Floating control limits; they shift without a change in the process.

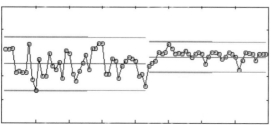

Figure 6.4B
Control limits should only shift after the process has changed.

Note that specification limits aren't used on an X-bar chart. This is because the high and low readings could be out of specification limits, yet have an average falling within the control limits. A process that is in control is not necessarily in spec.

SPC software packages let you create control charts easily. These programs compute the range, average, control limits, chart scale, draw both the X-bar and the R charts from the data you enter, and flag out of control points as they occur.

6.2 Median charts

Some people prefer to use median as the measure of central tendency. Since they don't require calculations, they are easier to find than averages. For a median chart, just plot each reading and circle the one in the center. In addition, because these charts use individual readings, you can use spec limits. If you use median charts, be aware that they tend to have about 25% more statistical variance than averages do.

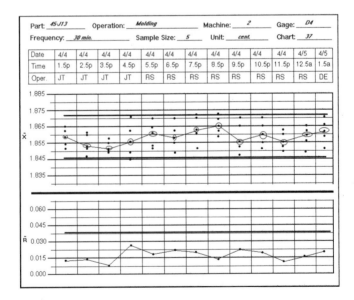

Figure 6.5
A median and range chart form

As with the X-bar chart, pair the median chart with a range chart for a complete picture of the process. The layout of the median and R chart is the same as the X-bar & R chart. Draw these charts on graph paper or on a special form as shown in Figure 6.5.

A tilde (~) is used to symbolize median. $\tilde{R}$ is the median of the range and $\tilde{X}$ is the median of the readings. $\tilde{\tilde{X}}$ is the median of the medians.

For this R chart, we calculate the sample ranges the same way we did before. In fact, the only difference in the range charts is that these limits use the median of the sample ranges instead of the average. To find the median of the ranges, sort all the range values from highest to lowest. The median is the value that falls in the middle. If you have an even number, add the two middle ranges and take their average. For example, if you have four sample ranges, 7, 5, 4, 2, you would have a median range of 4.5.

The upper and lower control limits use the same formulas as the sample ranges, except they use the median range instead of the average range.

$$UCL_R = D_4 * \tilde{R}$$

$$LCL_R = D_3 * \tilde{R}$$

For our sample, the $UCL_R = 2.282 * 4.5 = 12.69$. The $LCL_R = 0$ as the sample size was four, and there is no d_3 value for that sample size. A sample of the factors table can be found in Table 6.4 and a complete table of the factors can be found in Appendix C.

n	A_5	D_3	D_4
2	1.880	—	3.267
3	1.023	—	2.575
4	0.729	—	2.282

Table 6.4

For the median chart, we plot every reading on the chart instead of computing the average of each sample. Then we circle the point that falls in the middle of that sample. Again, when there is an even number of points, add the middle two values and take the average. For

Sample	1	2	3	4	5	6	7	8	9	10
Med.	2.18	2.61	2.65	2.49	2.5	2.18	2.61	2.58	2.54	2.54
Range	0.3	0.3	0.29	0.65	0.5	0.3	0.3	0.79	0.39	0.35

Sample	11	12	13	14	15	16	17	18	19	20
Med.	2.18	2.61	2.57	2.54	2.61	2.45	2.58	2.63	2.54	2.75
Range	0.3	0.3	0.54	0.23	0.3	0.53	0.79	0.74	0.39	0.2

Table 6.5

example, we'd plot each of the readings in our sample 1, 5, 6, 9, and circle the median of 5 + 6 / 2 = 5.5.

Use the first 20 to 25 samples to calculate trial control limits. The center limit equals the median of the medians. You will need the median of the ranges to find the control limits for the median chart.

The formula for the upper and lower control limits are:

$$UCL_{\tilde{X}} = \overline{\overline{X}} + (\overline{\tilde{A}}_2 * \overline{R})$$
$$LCL_{\tilde{X}} = \overline{\overline{X}} - (\overline{\tilde{A}}_2 * \overline{R})$$

For our 20 samples, we would have the median values shown in Table 6.5.

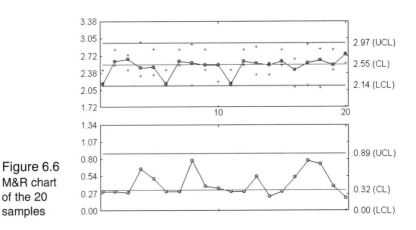

Figure 6.6
M&R chart
of the 20
samples

The median range is 0.325. The $UCL_R = 2.575 * 0.325 = .8369$ and the $LCL_R = 0$. The $\widetilde{\overline{X}}$ is 2.555. The $UCL_X = 2.555 + (1.265 * 0.325) = 2.9661$ and the $LCL_X = 2.555 - 0.4111 = 2.1439$. Figure 6.6 shows the median & R chart created from this data.

Set the scale for these charts as you would for the X-bar. For our 20 samples, the R chart scale is $1.255 - 0$ and the median chart scale is $3.38 - 1.73$.

6.3 s charts

You may want to pair an X-bar with an s chart (sigma chart) instead of a range chart. This is especially true if you use large sample sizes, because a range's accuracy decreases as the sample size increases. The s chart uses standard deviation to determine the spread of a sample. Unlike range, which we base on the extreme values, standard deviation reflects all the readings in a sample. However, standard deviation is harder to calculate.

For this chart we use a small 's' to represent the standard deviation of a sample. The Greek letter sigma (σ) represents the standard deviation for an entire population. An s chart provides a magnified image of a σ chart, *but don't plot one for the other; they aren't interchangeable.* We use an s-bar ($\bar{s}$) to symbolize the average of the standard deviations.

To create an s chart, first find the standard deviation of the samples. The formula for an s chart is:

$$s = \sqrt{\frac{(X_1 - \overline{X})^2 + (X_2 - \overline{X})^2 + (X_3 - \overline{X})^2 ... (X_n - \overline{X})^2}{n - 1}}$$

where, X_1, X_2, etc. = individual readings, $\overline{X}$ = the average of all the readings in the sample, n = the total number of readings. For example, the standard deviation for 3, 5, 7, 8, 4, 2, 4, 1, 2 is:

$$\overline{X} = 3 + 5 + 7 + 8 + 4 + 2 + 4 + 1 + 2 = 36 / 9 = 4$$

$$s = \sqrt{\dfrac{\begin{array}{c}(3 - 4)^2 + (5 - 4)^2 + (7 - 4)^2 + (8 - 4)^2 + \\ (4 - 4)^2 + (2 - 4)^2 + (4 - 4)^2 + (1 - 4)^2 + (2 - 4)^2\end{array}}{9 - 1}} =$$

$$\sqrt{\dfrac{(-1)^2 + (1)^2 + (3)^2 + (4)^2 + (0)^2 + (-2)^2 + (0)^2 + (-3)^2 + (-2)^2}{8}} =$$

$$\sqrt{\dfrac{1 + 1 + 9 + 16 + 0 + 4 + 0 + 9 + 4}{8}} = \sqrt{44 / 8} =$$

$$\sqrt{5.5} = 2.345$$

We would then plot the 2.345 on the s chart. To find the control limits for the s chart, we need the average of the standard deviations. For this we add the standard deviation of each sample and divide the total by the number of samples used. The formula is:

where s_1, s_2, etc. = the sample standard deviations and r = the number of samples used.

$$\overline{s} = \dfrac{s_1 + s_2 + s_3 \ldots s_\#}{r}$$

Use the s-bar value for the center limit. To calculate the upper and lower control limits we use B factors. A sample of B factors appears in Table 6.6, with a more complete listing in Appendix C.

n	A_5	B_3	B_4
2	2.659	—	3.267
3	1.954	—	2.568
4	1.628	—	2.266

Table 6.6

The formulas for the s chart control limits are:

$$UCL_s = B_4 * \bar{s}$$
$$LCL_s = B_3 * \bar{s}$$

The control limits for the X-bar chart use the s-bar value instead of the R-bar. The formulas for the X-bar chart are:

$$UCL_x = \bar{\bar{X}} + A_3 * \bar{s}$$
$$LCL_x = \bar{\bar{X}} - A_3 * \bar{s}$$

We can create an s chart from the same data used for the X-bar, median, and R charts. With the 20 samples shown in Table 6.7, we would have the following limits for the s chart: center line = 0.222, $UCL_S = 2.568 * 0.222 = 0.570$, and $LCL_S = 0$. And for the X-bar chart our limits are: center line = 2.536, $UCL_S = 2.536 + (1.954 * 0.222) = 2.536 + 0.4338 = 2.970$ and $LCL_S = 2.536 - 0.4338 = 2.102$.

The X-bar and s charts from this data appear in Figure 6.7.

We've looked at ways to study the variation in samples from a universe, which in this case is our process. For some processes, however, we'll want to know the standard deviation of the entire universe. Knowing this helps us judge the on-going quality of long-term and continuous processes.

Sample	1	2	3	4	5	6	7	8	9	10
Avg.	2.26	2.663	2.613	2.6	2.567	2.26	2.663	2.557	2.61	2.443
s	0.17	0.16	0.15	0.34	0.26	0.17	0.16	0.4	0.2	0.19

Sample	11	12	13	14	15	16	17	18	19	20
Avg.	2.26	2.663	2.603	2.49	2.663	2.407	2.557	2.53	2.61	2.697
s	0.17	0.16	0.27	0.12	0.16	0.27	0.4	0.38	0.2	0.11

Table 6.7

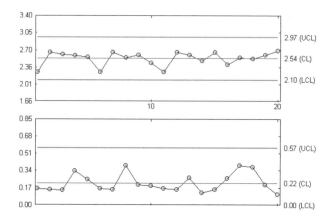

Figure 6.7
X-bar & s chart

6.4　Using sample variation
　　　to determine process variation

Both the $\overline{R}$ and the $\overline{s}$ lead us to estimates of the standard deviation of the universe (σ). In a normal distribution these sample averages have a direct relationship to σ. However, both fall slightly under the estimated σ. There are formulas for estimating σ from either the R or s values for greater accuracy.

We compute σ from the $\overline{R}$ value with the following formula:

$$\sigma = \overline{R} / d_2$$

Using the R value from our 20 samples, the $\sigma = 0.4245 / 1.693 = 0.2507$.

To compute σ from the $\overline{s}$ value, use the following formula:

$$\sigma = \overline{s} / c_4$$

Using the $\overline{s}$ value from the 20 samples, the $\sigma = 0.222 / 0.886 = 0.1967$. A sample of the d_2 and c_4 factors are shown in Table 6.8 with a full table in Appendix C.

n	d_2	c_4
2	1.128	0.798
3	1.693	0.886
4	2.059	0.921

Table 6.8

7.0 Process capability studies

I know of no way of judging the future
but by the past.

Patrick Henry

7.1 Natural tolerance vs. engineering tolerance

In Chapter 6 we based the control limits for our charts on the performance of the process rather than process specs. The main reason for this is specs apply to individual measurements, while the charts signal changes in statistics. A control chart sample may be within spec limits, yet have a reading outside these boundaries.

Using specs on a control chart also discourages improving beyond the spec range. Once we've met the required specs, we have no reason to continue improving our process. We forget specs are artificial or negotiated numbers, so we don't see that the process can improve.

Specs provide us with a guide to the customer's requirements, in the form of a tolerance range. They are the engineering tolerance of a measurement. While they are sometimes based on specific product or process needs, it is just as likely they are arbitrary. They can tell us if our final output is acceptable, but they can't tell us what the process is actually producing.

Instead of using specs, we use information from the control chart to find the natural operating range of the process. We call this the natural tolerance of the process. When the process distribution is normal, or nearly so, these tolerances fall three standard deviations on either side of the process average.

Natural tolerances form the area where we expect the process to produce 99.73% of its output. Figure 7.1 shows how engineering tolerances can differ from natural tolerances.

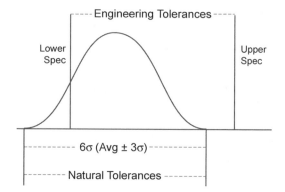

Figure 7.1
Engineering tolerances
and natural tolerances
aren't the same.

To find the natural tolerances of a process, we need to know its standard deviation. As discussed in Chapter 6, the standard deviation of the process (σ) has a direct relationship to the $\overline{R}$ or $\overline{s}$. If we use range, we use $\overline{R} / d_2$ to estimate σ. To estimate σ from s, we use $\overline{s} / c_4$. The d_2 and c_4 factors are found in Appendix C.

The natural tolerances are three standard deviations from the average or $\overline{\overline{X}} \pm 3\sigma$.

If we use the 20 samples from the X-bar & R chart we created in Chapter 6, the $\sigma = 0.4245 / 1.693 = 0.2507$. Since the X-bar = 2.536 and $3\sigma = 0.7521$, the natural tolerance range = 3.2881 – 1.7839.

For these formulas, the distribution of individual measurements needs a normal distribution or one close to it. One way to see if the distribution is normal is to create a histogram of the data. How is the data distributed? Does it have a normal curve? If the distribution isn't normal, and we try to apply the natural tolerances, the tolerance range won't show us where 99.73% of the values will fall.

7.2   Six-Sigma Quality

By the late 1970's, the West received a startling "wake-up call" for its complacent attitude toward quality. The quality improvement techniques that the U.S. so successfully exported to countries like

Japan, Korea and Singapore began to manifest themselves in the form of intense economic competition and superior products.

Technology giant Motorola Inc. responded with a top-to-bottom analysis of its business operations. The company adopted a rigorous set of processes known as Six Sigma that strives for zero-defects performance to ensure total customer satisfaction. Companies such as GE, Boeing, Kodak, Sony and Allied Signal have saved millions of dollars using Six Sigma techniques.

Motorola's assumption was that *average processes* operate at a three sigma level. In contrast, *best-in-class processes* perform at six sigma (see Table 7.1). The very disciplined, data-driven Six Sigma approach requires that companies follow a road map in which it defines defects, measures processes, analyzes process capability and improves them from the shop floor to the back office. If no process exists or if existing processes are deemed beyond repair, then Six Sigma methods are used to create effective and efficient processes.

Six Sigma Quality relies on a rigid organizational structure to ensure success. There is a *Quality Leader* or *Quality Manager* that represents the quality interests of all departments within the company. *Master Black Belts* are assigned to a specific area or function of the business: for example, human resources, order entry or shipping. *Process Owners* are exactly what the title implies; they are the individuals responsible for a specific process on a day-to-day basis. Process Owners and Master Black Belts work very closely and share information daily. Black Belts work full-time to lead a functional quality project through completion. They typically handle four to six projects a year with savings of roughly $225,000 per project and they devote a significant amount of time to coaching Green Belts. *Green Belts* are employees trained in Six Sigma who work part-time on Six Sigma assignments, but maintain their regular workload and responsibilities.

3σ	6σ
99.73% defect free	99.999% defect free
66,000 defects per million	3.4 defects per million

Table 7.1
Comparing average processes to best-in-class processes

Six Sigma Quality is a massive undertaking that involves radical innovation and change in organizational culture and requires corporate endorsement and financial backing. When properly implemented, the approach provides tangible business results that can be directly traced to the bottom line.

7.3 Calculating the percent out of spec

After we find the natural tolerance, we can use the estimated σ and $\overline{\overline{X}}$ to estimate how much of our product falls outside the spec limits. We begin by calculating how far the spec limits are from the process average. The formula for this is:

$$(USL - \overline{\overline{X}}) / \sigma \quad \text{and} \quad (LSL - \overline{\overline{X}}) / \sigma$$

The results of these calculations are known as Z scores, which we use with the Normal Table. The values in this table tell us what percent of our product is out of spec. Table 7.2 shows a sample of this table, with a complete table found in Appendix D.

Z	.09	.08	.07	.06	.05	.04	.03	.02	.01	.00	Z
-3.1	.00071	.00074	.00076	.00079	.00082	.0085	.00087	.00090	.00094	.00097	3.1
-3.0	.00100	.00104	.00107	.00111	.00114	.00118	.00122	.00126	.00131	.00135	3.0
-2.9	.0014	.0014	.0015	.0015	.0016	.0016	.0017	.0017	.0018	.0019	2.9

Table 7.2

If the specs for our 20 samples are 2.55 $\pm$ 0.75, our Z scores would be:

Upper Z score =
$(3.3 - 2.536) / 0.2507 = 3.0475$

Lower Z score =
$(1.8 - 2.536) / 0.2507 =$
-2.9358

The chart value for 3.05 is 0.00114, which is 0.114% out

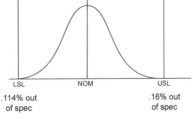

Figure 7.2
Out-of-spec percentages for our 20 samples

of spec. The value for -2.94 is 0.0016, or 0.16% out of spec. Figure 7.2 shows this calculation.

7.4 Impact of non-normal distributions

The Normal Table gives us percentages for distributions that are normal or nearly normal. If we assume a process is normal and it isn't, we'll get invalid data from the table. Figure 7.3 shows the actual and assumed distributions of a non-normal process. In this case, assuming the process is normal means we assume all of our product is in spec. In fact, about a third of our product is out of spec.

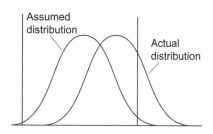

Figure 7.3
Two distributions with the same standard deviation. Note the percent out of spec is based on the assumption of normality.

Assuming our process is normal may cause us to adjust the process incorrectly. We can avoid this by constructing a histogram to check the distribution before we attempt a capability study.

7.5 Common capability and performance indexes

Comparing a set of specs to the natural tolerance of our process shows us how well an in-control process meets the requirements. The C_p and C_{pk} are *capability indexes* which make this comparison easy. Both indexes are ratios of the natural tolerance to the specs. The simplest of these is the C_p index.

The C_p index is the capability of the process. It refers to how well the process can satisfy the specs. It is the range of the specs divided by the six sigma spread or the natural tolerance ($\pm 3\sigma$).

The formula is:

$$C_p = \frac{ET}{NT} = \frac{USL - LSL}{6\sigma}$$

where ET = the engineering tolerance or specs, and NT = the natural tolerance.

Using our earlier sample:

$$C_p = \frac{3.3 - 1.8}{6\,(.2506)} = 0.9972$$

If we have a C_p index of one, the natural tolerance is the same width as the specs. A C_p index of two means the process is capable of producing parts with half the variability allowed by the specs. If the C_p is 0.5, the process has twice the variability needed to produce parts in spec. The larger the C_p value, the better the capability.

This index compares the spread of the specs to that of the natural tolerance. However, it doesn't tell us how centered the process is. C_p remains the same, regardless of the center line's location or how much product is out of spec. It only responds to changes in the process variability.

Process centering is also important, since a poorly centered process makes more out of spec parts than a well centered one. We use the C_{pk} index to measure process centering. This index is the range from the process average to the nearest spec limit divided by half the natural tolerance. Its formula is:

$$C_{pk} = \text{minimum of} \quad \frac{USL - \overline{\overline{X}}}{3\sigma} \quad \text{or} \quad \frac{\overline{\overline{X}} - LSL}{3\sigma}$$

For our example:

$$\text{Upper} = \frac{3.3 - 2.536}{3\,(0.2507)} = 1.0158$$

$$\text{Lower} = \frac{2.536 - 1.8}{3\,(0.2507)} = 0.97859$$

The C_{pk} is 0.97859, because that is the minimum value.

Because C_{pk} is the limit closest to the average, it gives us the worst end of the process. If its value is greater than one, everything is within spec limits. If it's between zero and one some parts are out of spec. If it's negative, the process average is out of spec.

The C_{pk} tells us how centered the process is, but it doesn't show us how the process will improve if it becomes more centered. To understand what the process is doing and what it can do, we need both the C_p and C_{pk} indexes. The C_p tells us if the process could fit the tolerances, and the C_{pk} tells us if it does. If both indexes are the same, the process is completely centered. Also, the C_{pk} will never be greater than the C_p.

Figure 7.4 shows the capability chart for our 20 samples. Here the C_p and C_{pk} values are nearly equal, and the process is nearly centered.

Comparing the capability data to the histogram gives us a better sense of what our process can do. Both studies estimate sigma for the population. Sometimes these agree and sometimes they don't. A process in statistical control with a nearly normal distribution will have similar sigma values for both. If the data is non-normal, skewed or out of control, the sigma values will be very different.

Don't be in a hurry to obtain a capability index. Many people err in basing a capability index from control chart information before they find out if the process is stable. Capability represents the fit between

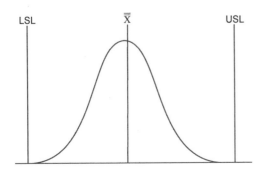

Figure 7.4
With C_p and C_{pk} almost equal, the process is nearly centered.

the expected future production and the specs. If we can't predict the process behavior, the capability means nothing.

We have just seen how the process capability index measures capability for an in-control process. Similarly, *process performance indexes* calculate the performance for processes that may or may not be in statistical control at any point in time. The performance index describes the distribution of product that was actually manufactured and shipped to customers. However, since the process is not necessarily in control, there is no assurance that future production will follow the same distribution.

Performance indexes are calculated the same way as capability indexes except that the overall standard deviation for the time period, s, is used instead of the short-term standard deviation, σ:

$$\sigma_s = \sqrt{\sum_{i=1}^{n} \frac{(x_i - \overline{X})^2}{n-1}}$$

where X_i is an individual reading, $\overline{X}$ is the average of the individual readings and n = the total number of all readings.

P_p is the performance index for process variation due just to common causes. It is expressed as:

$$P_p = \frac{USL - LSL}{6\sigma_s}$$

P_{pk} is the performance index for process variation and process centering due to common *and* special causes. The formula is:

$$P_{pk} = \text{the minimum of } \frac{USL - \overline{X}}{3\sigma_s} \text{ or } \frac{\overline{X} - LSL}{3\sigma_s}$$

Both P_p and P_{pk} should only be used to check against C_p and C_{pk} and to measure and prioritize improvement over time.

8.0 Control chart analysis

Probability is the very guide to life.

Thomas Hobbes

8.1 Detecting patterns

Patterns appear on a control chart when a process is not random. This behavior occurs when a special cause acts on the process. If its cause improves the process, you'll want to make it permanent. If not, you'll want to eliminate it. Detecting a pattern is the first step to finding a cause of variation.

With a normal curve about 68% of the samples fall within $\pm 1\sigma$, 95% within $\pm 2\sigma$ and 99.73% within $\pm 3\sigma$. When this isn't true, the process isn't in control and we should see patterns on the chart. Some patterns are easily detected with a quick glance at the control chart. For others you'll need to look a little closer. Among the things to look for are:

- *Any one point outside the control limits.*
- *Seven points in a row on one side of the center line.*
- *Seven consecutive points with each point higher than the previous point.*
- *Seven consecutive points with each point lower than the previous point.*
- *Two out of three points beyond two sigma all on the same side of the center line.*
- *Two out of three points beyond two sigma—all on the same side of the center line.*

Figure 8.1 illustrates several of these tests.

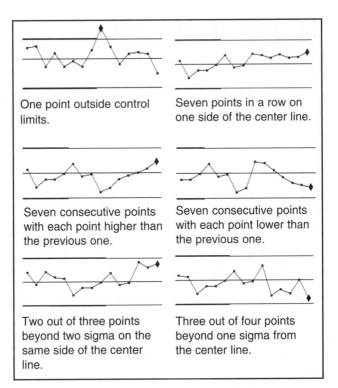

One point outside control limits.

Seven points in a row on one side of the center line.

Seven consecutive points with each point higher than the previous one.

Seven consecutive points with each point lower than the previous one.

Figure 8.1 Tests for non-random conditions

Two out of three points beyond two sigma on the same side of the center line.

Three out of four points beyond one sigma from the center line.

We also find non-random behavior by checking the number of runs on the chart. A run is a group of points on one side of the center line. Not enough runs shows a lack of variability which may indicate stratification. The data in Table 8.1, helps us determine if there are enough runs. When the number of runs is less than or equal to this number, the process isn't random.

Points above center line

	6	7	8	9	10	11	12	13	14
6	3	4	4	4	5	5	5	5	5
7	4	4	4	5	5	5	6	6	6
8	4	4	5	5	6	6	6	6	7
9	4	5	5	6	6	6	7	7	7

Points below center line

Table 8.1

These tests show how random the process is. However, they may not pick up other patterns that occur on your charts. And the more tests you run, the more likely you are to call the process out of control when it is in control. Each test increases this risk by about 5%.

8.2 Cycles

In control charts, cycles appear when variability increases in the overall output. A cycle on the control chart means something is changing over time and it influences the process. If you can identify the cycle's cause, you may be able to pinpoint which part of the cycle produces the best output. Then you'd want to control this cause to stabilize the output at this level. Figure 8.2 shows cycles on a control chart.

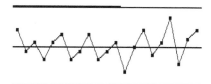

Figure 8.2
Control chart cycles

8.3 Trends

Like cycles, trends show that something is changing constantly. Toolwear or the evaporation of a solvent would show up as trends on a control chart. If the trend can't or shouldn't be controlled, you can use inclined control limits, as on a toolwear chart, to counteract it. The control chart in Figure 8.3 shows a trend.

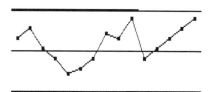

Figure 8.3
Control chart trend

8.4 Mixtures

Control charts often show mixtures when two or more process are analyzed as one. The output of two machines plotted on one chart is an example. A chart of two machines with different process centers may show point above and below the center line, but won't have many near it. Figure 8.4 shows a control chart of mixed data.

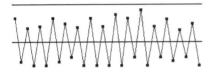

Figure 8.4
Mixed Data

Histograms also show mixtures. If there are two processes, the histogram will usually have two or more humps.

If you suspect mixed data, plot the points without the connecting lines. This will help you determine if the chart shows layering. Once you've found mixed data, you may want to plot a separate chart for each process or process level. Separate charts can help pinpoint the cause of the mixture.

8.5 Stratification

Stratified data, like mixed data, occurs when two or more processes are studied together and produces the same type of pattern. However, stratified data points appear to hug the center line. This occurs when each reading in a sample is taken from first one machine, then the second machine, and then back to the first machine. The second sample would begin with a reading from the second machine, then the first machine, and back to the second. In this case, each data point will reflect both machines, but every other

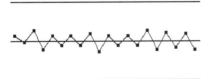

Figure 8.5
Stratified data

point will have two readings from the same machine. The result is the pattern shown in Figure 8.5.

Like mixed data, stratified data shows up in histograms. It also can be seen on the control chart if you plot data without connecting the lines.

8.6 Shifts

Shifts in the process also create a noticeable pattern. A shift is a sudden change in the pattern, such as a drop or jump. It can indicate a change in operators or new materials. For example, if the first operator runs the machine at set level and the next operator sets it a little higher,

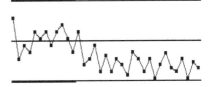

Figure 8.6
Process shift

you'd notice a shift in the X-bar pattern. Caused by different machine operators, this pattern would most likely repeat with each operator change. Figure 8.6 shows a shift pattern.

8.7 Instability

Unnaturally large fluctuations on the control chart show process instability. Points may be outside the limits on both sides of the center line. Overadjusting equipment, mixed lots of material, and differences in gages often cause instability. It also may be the result of several variables affecting one characteristic. Figure 8.7 shows an example of an unstable pattern.

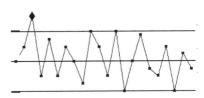

Figure 8.7
Unstable process

8.8 Bunching

Bunching occurs when a group of samples, which appear close to each other, have the same or very similar readings. This is shown in Figure 8.8. This type of pattern indicates a sudden change in the causes of variation. For example, a different person taking the readings, a temporary shift in the distribution, or recalibrating a gage.

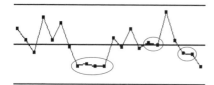

Figure 8.8
Process bunching

8.9 Freaks

Because they occur irregularly, freaks are often the most difficult pattern to eliminate. Freaks occur when one point goes outside control limits and then the process returns to its normal behavior. This is shown in Figure 8.9.

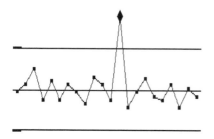

Figure 8.9
Control chart freak

Since they occur only once in a while, they are hard to duplicate. With just one sample out of control there is little data to analyze. Although it is tempting to ignore a single out of control point, especially if it is close to the control limits, freaks do indicate a problem in the process. When you ignore a freak you may be ignoring a change in the process.

Freaks can have any number of causes, the most common of which are measurement and plotting errors. Other causes include an incomplete operation, facility problem such as power surge or a breakdown, and occasional damage from handling. One way to track the cause of a freak is to make notes at each occurrence and compare them over time.

When you analyze control chart patterns, you'll find they often occur in both the range and X-bar charts. Look at the range chart pattern first. Eliminating a pattern from the range chart often eliminates it from the X-bar chart as well.

9.0 Measurement errors

*Mistakes live in the neighborhood of truth
and therefore delude us.*

Rabindranath Tagore

9.1 Accuracy, precision and predictability

SPC depends on the accuracy and precision of each reading. By accuracy we mean how close the average is to the target. Precision refers to how the readings spread out around the average value. For example, let's say you need to hire a bodyguard. Four bodyguards show up at a target range to prove their shooting ability. Figure 9.1 shows the results of this test. Which one would you hire?

The first applicant scattered his shots all over the target. He is neither precise nor accurate. Number two is accurate, but not very

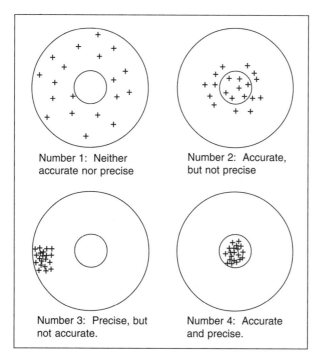

Number 1: Neither accurate nor precise

Number 2: Accurate, but not precise

Number 3: Precise, but not accurate.

Number 4: Accurate and precise.

Figure 9.1
Targets showing the difference between precision and accuracy

precise. Her shots scattered in and around the bull's eye. Judging from this target, she'd have about a 50% chance of hitting her target when it counted. Number three was precise, with each shot near the others, but he wasn't very accurate. From this example, it looks as though he wouldn't hit the target when he had to. There is no question about the final applicant, she is both precise and accurate. Her shots are close together and on target, so you decide to hire her.

When we take measurements, we'll find the same types of differences between different instruments and measuring techniques. For this reason, we expect some variance as a normal part of the measurement process. If we don't limit it, however, it will distort our control charts.

If we calibrate an instrument, we change its accuracy, but not its precision. Maintenance on an instrument effects its precision. Unnecessary service may cause a poor adjustment and increase the variability of the readings. You can use statistics to monitor your measurement system and show you when devices need adjusting. These techniques help limit the measurement variation and reduce control chart distortions.

9.2 Operator variability

The hardest variable to control in any measurement system is the operator. Factors such as attitude, fatigue, and comfort, affect a person's ability to repeat a process exactly each time. This is true when using a measurement device and even more so when asked to make a judgment call such as matching colors. Even the reading from a correctly used device has some variation.

How would you read the first dial shown in Figure 9.2? You could it read as 0.020, 0.025, 0.0225, or 0.022. Why is there a difference? It's a matter of interpretation. When the reading falls between two numbers, common practice is to estimate its actual value. Even when the divisions on the dial are in the tens of thousandths, we have to estimate the true value.

Looking at the second dial, we would say a mark slightly over 0.020 indicates a larger part than one with a reading slightly under 0.020. Now, suppose we know that the device's accuracy is plus or minus 0.005. Would we still say the larger reading was a larger part? How we read and interpret a device depends on our training, our experience—even our mood.

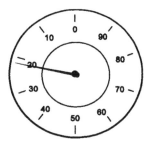

One way to reduce the impact of operator judgment calls is to use a device that measures one digit over the spec. For example, if the spec value goes to hundredths, the device should go to the thousandths. Operators then read the device to the nearest division without estimating values between divisions.

Another way to reduce the impact of operator variance is to use instruments with digital readouts. By providing the reading in numeric form, these devices eliminate judgment errors. Operators simply record the displayed value without any guessing.

Figure 9.2
Divisions to the thousandth provide more accurate interpretations than those to the hundredth.

9.3 Instructions

Instructions are another source of variation. How clearly you describe the steps for taking a measurement determines how accurate and precise it will be. How you describe a defect determines if it is identified and if a defective part is kept or rejected. Unclear instructions force operators to guess which method is correct. Each person may interpret them differently, providing you with a group of readings that resemble the first bodyguard's target.

For example, what would you do if you had the following instructions?

Check for proper operation.

"Check for proper operation" tells you what to do, but doesn't tell you how to do it. Suppose your instructions were:

To check for proper operation:

1. *Mount the unit in the test stand, securing the rear holds down first.*
2. *Connect the red wire on the base unit to the red wire inside the tube. Connect black wire to black wire.*
3. *Attach the pressure tube from the indicator. Screw tight and use the transducer to check for leaks.*
4. *Record any reading from the transducer on the check sheet. Reject any part registering 50 or higher.*

Now you not only know to check for proper operation, but you know *how to* check for proper operation. Even these instructions may not be clear enough for someone unfamiliar with the equipment. You can use diagrams or add other points as needed to further clarify the steps.

The goal is to ensure each person makes the same readings, with the greatest chance of duplicating them. Operators change, vacations require others to fill in, and operating practices get sloppy over time if the instructions are not clear from the beginning.

9.4 Manual inspection problems

There are no instruments for some types of inspection. The only tools are the inspector's own senses. For example, color characteristics and surface defects, such as marks and scratches, depend on visual inspection. Other features, such as odor, also rely on a person's senses.

With these types of inspections, explaining what is and is not acceptable is difficult. Standard boards, showing both good and bad examples, provide all inspectors with a standard basis for their decisions. Comparing parts to the standard boards helps reduce variance between inspectors. It does not, however, eliminate it.

As discussed earlier in this chapter, attitude, comfort, and fatigue affect a person's work. This is most evident in manual inspections. For instance, as workers become fatigued, their perceptions change. They may become more critical, or they may let more defects slide by. Some people think if they don't reject some parts, they aren't doing their job. They become more critical as the number of defective parts decreases keeping rejects at the same level. This hides benefits from improvements in the process.

There is no good way to prevent this type of shift in manual inspection. You can find these changes by passing a fixed number of known defective parts by the inspectors at regular intervals. If the number of defects they find differs significantly, workers may need more training. Control charts can help with this, as well as with tracking differences in inspection practices. For example, you could ask each inspector to examine a control group of a part. Then plot their findings on a p or u chart (See Chapter 10). Those inspectors whose results fall outside the limits are inspecting differently enough to warrant attention.

9.5 Repeatability & reproducibility

Gage capability studies help us determine gage accuracy and operator precision. A repeatability study helps us find gage variation. For this study, one person measures the same dimension several times with the same device. Reproducibility studies show us variation between operators and requires more than one person to measure the same dimension with the same gage.

Gage R&R studies usually use 2 or 3 operators who take 2 or 3 readings of each part. To conduct a gage repeatability and reproducibility (Gage R&R) study:

Step 1:

For this study, our sample groups must consist of like parts. Have each operator measure each part with the same gage and record each measurement. For a two-trial study they need to measure the same parts in the same order with the same gage again. If it's a three-trial study, you'll need a third set of measurements. Table 9.1 shows data from a three-trial study with three operators.

Table 9.1
Gage R&R Data Sheet

	OPERATOR/ TRIAL #	PART										AVG
		1	2	3	4	5	6	7	8	9	10	
1	Opr A Trial 1	1.295	1.267	1.243	1.295	1.274	1.285	1.243	1.292	1.266	1.276	
2	2	1.295	1.267	1.243	1.295	1.273	1.286	1.245	1.292	1.267	1.276	
3	3	1.292	1.267	1.247	1.294	1.274	1.289	1.242	1.292	1.268	1.273	
4	Average											$\overline{X}_a=$
5	Range											$\overline{R}_a=$
6	Opr B Trial 1	1.268	1.259	1.271	1.262	1.270	1.260	1.260	1.275	1.275	1.267	
7	2	1.273	1.259	1.269	1.263	1.268	1.261	1.260	1.276	1.275	1.267	
8	3	1.271	1.259	1.269	1.265	1.269	1.264	1.265	1.276	1.275	1.269	
9	Average											$\overline{X}_b=$
10	Range											$\overline{R}_b=$
11	Opr C Trial 1	1.296	1.268	1.296	1.274	1.286	1.244	1.293	1.266	1.266	1.277	
12	2	1.296	1.267	1.296	1.273	1.286	1.244	1.292	1.267	1.266	1.279	
13	3	1.294	1.266	1.293	1.276	1.290	1.244	1.294	1.267	1.266	1.279	
14	Average											$\overline{X}_c=$
15	Range											$\overline{R}_c=$
16	Part Avg ($\overline{X}_p$)											$\overline{\overline{X}}=$ $R_p=$
17	($\overline{R}_a+\overline{R}_b+\overline{R}_c$) /[# of operators = 3] =Rdouble bar											
18	Max $\overline{X}$ – Min $\overline{X}$ = $\overline{X}$DIFF =											
19*	Rdouble bar × D₄ = UCLᵣ =											
20*	Rdouble bar × D₃ = LCLᵣ =											

*D_4 = 3.27 for two trials and 2.58 for three trials; D_3 = 0 for up to seven trials. UCL_R represents the limit of individual R's. Circle those that are beyond this limit; identify the cause and correct. Repeat these readings using the same appraiser and unit as originally used or discard values and re-average and recompute R and the limiting value from the remaining observations.

Step 2:
Subtract the smallest reading from the largest reading in rows 1, 2 and 3; enter the result in row 5. Do the same for rows 6, 7 and 8; and 11, 12 and 13 and enter results in rows 10 and 15, respectively. (Entries in rows 5, 10 and 15 are made as positive values.)

Step 3:
Total row 5 and divide the total by the number of parts sampled to obtain the average range for the first operator's trials $\overline{R}_a$. Do the same for rows 10 and 15 to obtain $\overline{R}_b$ and $\overline{R}_c$.

Step 4:
Transfer the averages of rows 5, 10 and 15 to row 17. Add them together and divide by the number of operators and enter results Rdouble bar (average of all ranges).

Step 5:
Enter Rdouble bar in rows 19 and 20 and multiply by D_3 and D_4 to get the upper and lower control limits. Note D_3 is zero and D_4 is 3.27 if two trials are used. The value of the Upper Control Limit (UCL_R) of the individual ranges is entered in row 19. The Lower Control Limit (LCL_R) for less than seven trials is zero.

Step 6:
Repeat any readings that produced range greater than the calculated UCL_R using the same operator and part as originally used, or discard those values and re-average and recompute Rdouble bar and the limiting value UCL_R based upon the revised sample size. Correct the special cause that produced the out-of-control condition. If the data were plotted and analyzed using a control chart, this condition would have already been corrected and would not occur here.

Step 7:
Total rows 1, 2, 3, 6, 7, 8, 11, 12 and 13. Divide the sum in each row by the number of parts sampled and enter these values in the "Avg" column.

Step 8:
Add the averages in rows 1, 2 and 3 and divide the total by the

number of trials and enter the value in row 4 in the $\overline{X}_a$ block. Repeat this procedure for rows 6, 7, and 8; and 11, 12 and 13, and enter the results in the cells for $\overline{X}_b$ and $\overline{X}_c$ in rows 9 and 14, respectively.

Step 9:
Enter the maximum and minimum averages of rows 4, 9 and 14 in the appropriate space in row 18 and determine the differences. Enter this difference in the space labeled $\overline{X}_{DIFF}$ in row 18.

Step 10:
Total the measurements for each trial for each part, and divide the total by the number of measurements (number of trials times the

	OPERATOR/ TRIAL #	PART										AVG
		1	2	3	4	5	6	7	8	9	10	
1	Opr A Trial 1	1.295	1.267	1.243	1.295	1.274	1.285	1.243	1.292	1.266	1.276	1.2736
2	2	1.295	1.267	1.243	1.295	1.273	1.286	1.245	1.292	1.267	1.276	1.2739
3	3	1.292	1.267	1.247	1.294	1.274	1.289	1.242	1.292	1.268	1.273	1.2738
4	Average	1.294	1.267	1.244	1.295	1.274	1.287	1.243	1.292	1.267	1.275	$\overline{X}_a$=1.2738
5	Range	0.003	0.000	0.004	0.001	0.001	0.004	0.003	0.000	0.002	0.003	$\overline{R}_a$=0.0021
6	Opr B Trial 1	1.268	1.259	1.271	1.262	1.270	1.260	1.260	1.275	1.275	1.267	1.2667
7	2	1.273	1.259	1.269	1.263	1.268	1.261	1.260	1.276	1.275	1.267	1.2671
8	3	1.271	1.259	1.269	1.265	1.269	1.264	1.265	1.276	1.275	1.269	1.2682
9	Average	1.271	1.259	1.270	1.263	1.269	1.262	1.262	1.276	1.275	1.268	$\overline{X}_b$=1.2675
10	Range	0.005	0.000	0.002	0.003	0.002	0.004	0.005	0.001	0.000	0.002	$\overline{R}_b$=0.0024
11	Opr C Trial 1	1.296	1.268	1.296	1.274	1.286	1.244	1.293	1.266	1.266	1.277	1.2766
12	2	1.296	1.267	1.296	1.273	1.286	1.244	1.292	1.267	1.266	1.279	1.2766
13	3	1.294	1.266	1.293	1.276	1.290	1.244	1.294	1.267	1.266	1.279	1.2769
14	Average	1.295	1.267	1.295	1.274	1.287	1.244	1.293	1.267	1.266	1.278	$\overline{X}_c$=1.2766
15	Range	0.002	0.002	0.003	0.003	0.004	0.000	0.002	0.001	0.000	0.002	$\overline{R}_c$=0.0019
16	Part Avg ($\overline{X}_p$)	1.2867	1.2643	1.2697	1.2774	1.2767	1.2641	1.2661	1.2781	1.2693	1.2737	$\overline{\overline{X}}$=1.27261 R_p=0.0226
17	([$\overline{R}_a$=0.0021] +[$\overline{R}_b$=0.0024] +[$\overline{R}_c$=0.0019]) /[# of appraisers = 3] =											0.0021
18	[Max $\overline{X}$ = 1.2766] – [Min $\overline{X}$ = 1.2675] = $\overline{X}_{DIFF}$ =											0.0091
19*	[Rdouble bar = 0.0021] × [D₄ = 2.58] = UCL$_R$ =											0.0054
20*	[Rdouble bar = 0.0021] × [D₃ =0.00] = LCL$_R$ =											0.0000

Table 9.2
Completed Gage R&R Data Sheet

number of operators). Enter the results in row 16 in the space provided for part average.

Step 11:
Subtract the smallest part average from the largest part average and enter the result in the space labeled R_p in row 16. R_p is the range of part averages.

Step 12:
Transfer the calculated values of Rdouble bar, X_{DIFF} and R_p to the cells provided. A completed Gage R&R Data Sheet is shown in Table 9.2.

Step 13:
Perform the calculation for *Repeatability: Equipment Variation (EV)* using the formula and K_1 factors from Table 9.3:

$$EV = \text{Rdouble bar} \times K_1$$
$$= 0.00213 \times 3.05$$
$$= 0.0064965 = 0.007$$

Step 14:
Perform the calculation for *Reproducibility: Appraiser Variation (AV)* using the formula:

$$AV = \sqrt{(\overline{X}_{DIFF} \times K_2)^2 - (EV^2/nr)}$$

where

$$n = \text{number of parts}$$
$$r = \text{number of trials}$$

$$AV =$$

$$\sqrt{(0.0091 \times 2.70)^2 - (0.0065^2/(10 \times 3))}$$
$$= 0.0245356 = 0.025$$

K Factors for Gage R&R		
Trials	K_1	
2	4.56	
3	3.05	
Appraisers	2	3
K_2	3.65	2.70
Parts	K_3	
2	3.65	
3	2.70	
4	2.30	
5	2.08	
6	1.93	
7	1.82	
8	1.74	
9	1.67	
10	1.62	

Table 9.3

Step 15:
Perform the calculation for *Repeatability & Reproducibility (R&R)* using the formula:

$$R\&R = \sqrt{(EV^2 + AV^2)}$$
$$= \sqrt{(0.0065^2 + 0.02428^2)}$$
$$= 0.02513 = 0.025$$

Step 16:
Perform the calculation for *Part Variation (PV)* using the formula:

$$PV = R_p \times K_3$$
$$= 0.0226 \times 1.62$$
$$= 0.0366 = 0.037$$

Step 17:
Perform the calculation for *Total Variation (TV)* using the formula:

$$TV = \sqrt{R\&R^2 + PV^2}$$
$$= \sqrt{(0.02513)^2 + (0.0366)^2}$$
$$= 0.0443959 = 0.044$$

Step 18:
Perform the calculations for *% EV (Equipment Variation)* using the formula:

$$\% EV = 100\,[EV/TV]$$
$$= 100\,[0.007/0.045]$$
$$= 16\%$$

Step 19:
Perform the calculations for *% AV (Appraiser Variation)* using the formula:

$$\% AV = 100\,[AV/TV]$$
$$= 100\,[0.025/0.045]$$
$$= 56\%$$

Step 20:
Perform the calculations for *% R&R* using the formula:

$$\% \text{ R\&R} = 100 \text{ [R\&R/TV]}$$
$$= 100 \text{ [0.025/0.045]}$$
$$= 56\%$$

Step 21:
Perform the calculations for *% PV (Part Variation)* using the formula:

$$\% \text{ PV} = 100 \text{ [PV/TV]}$$
$$= 100 \text{ [0.037/0.045]}$$
$$= 82\%$$

10.0 Control charts for non-conforming attributes

Detect and fix any problem in a production process
at the lowest value stage possible.

Andrew S. Grove

10.1 Types of attribute data and charts

All the control charts we've looked at so far have been for measured data. With some parts or processes, it isn't possible or practical to measure data so these charts won't work. For example, a light bulb works or it doesn't. A motor will start or it won't. A paint job might have flaws in it or it might not. These characteristics produce attribute data and require control charts for attributes.

There are two types of attribute data, the number of *non-conforming units* and the number of *non-conformities*. Go/no-go data is non-conforming. For example, a light bulb is good or bad. The bulb either conforms to the requirements or it does not. In a group of 100 light bulbs, you can't have more than 100 non-conforming items. We use 'p' and 'np' charts to plot the number of non-conforming parts in a group.

The number of non-conformities is a count of defects on a part or product. For example, a paint job could have several marks on it. Each mark counts as a non-conformity. As a result, a group of 100 parts could have an unlimited number of non-conformities. Since this type of attribute data is different, it requires different charts— 'c' and 'u' charts. We will look at these in greater detail in the next chapter.

Both types of attribute charts offer chart choices for fixed sample sizes or varying sample sizes. Keep in mind that chart calculations

	Chart for varying sample size	*Chart for constant sample size*
Chart for no. of non-conforming	p	np
Chart for no. of non-conformities	u	c

Table 10.1

are easier if the samples are all the same size. Table 10.1 shows which chart to use for each option.

10.2   p charts

Let's begin with the charts for non-conforming units. This type of go/no-go outcome follows the laws of binomial distribution we discussed in Chapter 2. Whether the motor starts, or it doesn't is the same as our card deck sample. The card is red or black, the bulb lights or it doesn't, the coin is heads or tails—there are no other options. X-bar chart calculations would not work with this data.

We can, however, calculate limits that give us the same assurance as the three sigma limits on the X-bar chart. Instead of plotting the average value, we plot a percentage (p) of non-conforming units. Sometimes called fraction non-conforming, this calculation estimates the average number of non-conforming units the process makes.

As mentioned in the previous section, the sample size may vary on the p chart. If each sample consists of a day's production, the daily count will likely change from day to day. We can use varying sample sizes because the p chart lets us calculated new limits for each point.

To create a p chart:

Step 1: Find the fraction non-conforming (p) for each sample and plot these values on the chart.

After plotting the points, draw a line connecting them. Note that the chart scale should be about twice the largest p value.

The formula for the fraction non-conforming (p) is:

$$\frac{\text{Number of non-conforming units}}{\text{Number inspected}}$$

For example, Table 10.2 shows 10 samples and their p values.

Sample	Defective	Inspected	p
1	22	321	0.0685
2	15	254	0.0591
3	18	435	0.0414
4	32	675	0.0474
5	14	202	0.0693
6	35	845	0.0414
7	12	231	0.0519
8	27	513	0.0526
9	10	178	0.0562
10	20	785	0.0255

Step 2: Find the average p value ($\bar{p}$).
The formula is:

$$\bar{p} = \frac{\text{Total non-conforming units}}{\text{Total units inspected}}$$

Table 10.2

For our example, $\bar{p}$ equals:

$$225 / 4439 = 0.05069$$

Step 3: Calculate the upper control limit for a point.

The upper control limit formula is:

$$UCL_p = \bar{p} + 3\sqrt{\frac{\bar{p}\,(1-\bar{p})}{n}}$$

where n = the number of units inspected for a sample.

For the first point of our example the upper control limit is:

$$0.05069 + 3\sqrt{\frac{0.05069\,(1-0.05069)}{321}} = 0.08742$$

Step 4: Calculate the lower control limit for that point.
The formula for the lower control limit is:

$$LCL_p = \bar{p} - 3\sqrt{\frac{\bar{p}\ (1-\bar{p})}{n}}$$

where n = the number of units inspected for a sample.

We can't have less than zero non-conforming parts. If we get a negative number, the lower control limit is zero.

For the first point of our example, the lower control limit is:

$$0.05069 - 0.03673 = 0.01396$$

Step 5: Repeat Steps 3 and 4 for each point.
Table 10.3 shows the upper and lower control limits for each of our ten samples.

Sample	UCL	LCL
1	0.08742	0.01396
2	0.09198	0.00940
3	0.08224	0.01914
4	0.07602	0.02536
5	0.09699	0.00439
6	0.07333	0.02805
7	0.09400	0.00739
8	0.07973	0.02165
9	0.10019	0.00155
10	0.07418	0.02720

Step 6: Draw the control limits on the chart.
The p-bar value is the center line. Figure 10.1 shows a p chart from this data.

We adjust the width of the control limits to reflect the amount of error we expect from our samples. The value we expect does not change when the sample size changes, but there is a change in the amount of error. If our sample size is large, the p value is closer to the true value than if the sample size is small. This is why we move the limits out for smaller samples and in for large ones.

Table 10.3

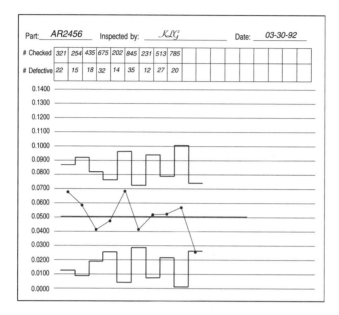

Figure 10.1
p chart from
our example

If the sample size only varies slightly, we can average the sample size and use the same limits for the entire chart. If a point falls near a limit, we need to find the actual limits for that point. This allows us to verify if it is in control or not. Another option is to average the sample sizes and use the np chart formulas for our limits.

To analyze p charts, we use the same pattern analysis techniques that we use for X-bar charts.

10.3 np charts

The np chart is a form of the p chart. These charts replace p charts when the sample size is constant.

For the p chart, we plotted a fraction of the non-conforming units. With the np chart, however, we use the actual number of these units. The actual number of non-conforming parts is often easier to understand than a percentage. Therefore, if the sample size is constant or nearly so, use the np chart. The np chart is also easier to create because it has a constant set of control limits.

To create an np chart:

Step 1: Find the average np value ($\overline{np}$).
The formula is:

$$\overline{np} = \frac{\text{Total non-conforming units}}{\text{Total units inspected}}$$

For example, let's say we inspect 75 parts in every lot. For the first 15 samples we find the following numbers of non-conforming parts: 23, 19, 34, 26, 21, 23, 30, 25, 16, 28, 31, 33, 17, 15, 22. The total non-conforming is 363 and we inspected 1,125. Our p-bar value is 0.32267.

Step 2: Calculate the center line value, $\overline{np}$.
The formula is $(n * \overline{p})$.

For our example, n = 75 and $\overline{p}$ = 0.32267

$$n\overline{p} = 24.20$$

Step 3: Find the upper control limit.
The formula for the upper control limit is:

$$\text{UCL}_{np} = n\overline{p} + 3 \sqrt{n\overline{p} \ (1 - \overline{p})}$$

For our example, the UCL is:

$$24.20025 + 3 \sqrt{24.20025 \ (1 - 0.32267)} = 38.71833$$

Step 4: Find the lower control limit.
The formula for the lower control limit is:

$$\text{LCL}_{np} = n\overline{p} - 3 \sqrt{n\overline{p} (1 - \overline{p})}$$

For our example, the LCL is 24.20025 – 14.51808 = 9.68217.

Step 5: Plot the actual number of non-conforming units for each sample and draw the control limits.

Note that the scale should be set so the upper control limit falls about two thirds of the way up the chart.

Figure 10.2 shows an np chart for the data in our example.

We can use the p or np chart for more than non-conformities. For example, if you bulk mail 2,000 marketing flyers monthly, you could use an np chart to track the responses. If the number of flyers you send varies each month, you'd use a p chart to track responses.

Whether you use a p or np chart, you'll need to make the sample size large enough to ensure there is at least one non-conforming unit in each sample. If not, you'll lose the ability to detect process improvements. A good rule of thumb is to set the sample size so n times $\bar{p}$ is at least 5.

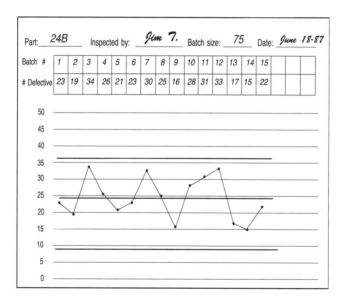

Figure 10.2
np chart

11.0 Control charts for the number of non-conformities

It is the quality rather than quantity that matters.

Publius Syrus

The second type of attribute data is the number of non-conformities. As mentioned in Chapter 10, this type of data is a count of the defects on a part or group of parts. Defects may include scratches, dents, stains, chips, etc. grouped together or just one defect type for each chart. For this type of attribute study, we use a count of the total defects per unit even if one defect is enough to reject the unit. We use a 'c' or a 'u' chart to study this type of data.

11.1 c charts

To study this type of attribute data we use the Poisson distribution and, for c charts, we have a constant sample size. Poisson distributions, as discussed in Chapter 2, are used for counts of events or occurrences in a unit. The unit may be a specific time frame, location or piece count.

For the c chart, your defects must meet three conditions. First, they must be independent of each other. For example, marks caused by handling are independent of those caused by flaws in the casting. Different marks caused by the same burr in the handling equipment have the same cause and are therefore not independent. Using data that isn't independent inflates control limits and distorts the study's results.

The second condition is that the defect is rare compared to how often it could occur. Let's say the burr in the handling equipment marks about one in 40 parts. It could, however, mark every part. The chance of any one part being marked is slight, so it meets the second condition.

The final condition is that the defects occur within a set time, area, or product. This could be a square yard of fabric, a group of 200 bolts, an entire car, or work from one shift. The c chart like the np chart deals with a sample size. With a fixed size unit, we can set the sample size at one unit, even if that unit has 1,000 parts.

Sample	Units	Defects
1	1	230
2	1	200
3	1	231
4	1	220
5	1	215
6	1	216
7	1	226
8	1	231
9	1	217
10	1	209
11	1	236
12	1	213
13	1	204
14	1	235
15	1	219
16	1	201
17	1	211
18	1	224
19	1	213
20	1	200

Table 11.1

To create a c chart:

Step 1: Define the inspection unit and collect data.

If your product is made with a fixed number per lot, one lot might be a good unit. If the product is a continuous or semi-continuous product, such as wire or sheet steel, the unit could be a set number of feet or yards. Other dimensions, such as width and thickness also must be constant.

Step 2: Find the average c value ($\bar{c}$).

The formula for $\bar{c}$ is:

c = No. of non-conformities in a sample

so $\bar{c} =$

$$\frac{\text{Total number of non-conformities}}{\text{Number of samples}}$$

For example, Table 11.1 shows 20 samples. The total number of defects is 4,351 and the unit size is one. The c-bar value is 4,351 / 20 = 217.55.

Step 3 : Calculate the upper control limit.
The upper control limit formula is:

$$UCL_c = \bar{c} + 3\sqrt{\bar{c}}$$

Since our sample has a fixed unit size of one, we'd calculate the upper control limit as:

$$217.55 + 3\sqrt{217.55} = 217.55 + 44.25 = 261.80$$

Step 4: Calculate the lower control limit.
The lower control limit formula is:

$$LCL_c = \bar{c} - 3\sqrt{\bar{c}}$$

We'd calculate the upper control limit for our sample as:

$$217.55 - 44.25 = 173.30$$

Step 5: Set the scale, plot the data and draw control limits.
Set the scale so the $\bar{c}$ value is in the middle of the chart. The lower scale value doesn't have to be zero, but you'll want to select a range

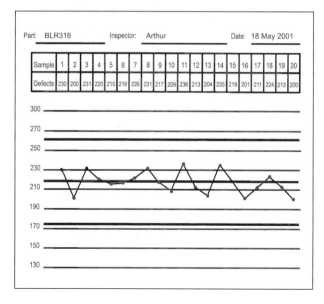

Part:	BLR316					Inspector:		Arthur					Date:		18 May 2001				

Sample	1	2	3	4	5	6	7	8	9	10	11	12	13	14	15	16	17	18	19	20
Defects	230	200	231	220	215	216	226	231	217	209	236	213	204	235	219	201	211	224	213	200

Figure 11.1
c chart from our sample data

that will include all probable data points. For our sample, this would put the maximum scale around 300 and the minimum around 130.

Figure 11.1 shows a c chart of our example.

11.2 u charts

Like the c chart, u charts use a Poisson distribution and therefore defects must meet the first two conditions. For the u chart, however, the sample size may vary from sample to sample. While each sample can have any number of units, each unit within a sample should be equal. For example, a sample could be of eight-ounce glasses but not eight and twelve-ounce glasses.

Because u chart samples can vary in size, their construction is like that of a p chart. Each sample has its own upper and lower control limits.

To create a u chart:

Step 1: Collect data and find the average number of defects per unit.
Use the following formula to find the average number of defects per unit:

$$u = \frac{\text{Number of defects in the sample}}{\text{Number of units in the sample}}$$

For example, Table 11.2 shows 15 samples, the number of units, the number of defects and their u value.

Sample	Units	Defects	u value
1	32	73	2.28
2	16	56	3.5
3	25	45	1.8
4	19	36	1.89
5	13	32	2.46
6	39	67	1.72
7	28	53	1.89
8	31	82	2.65
9	16	40	2.5
10	21	51	2.43
11	36	80	2.22
12	23	45	1.96
13	25	66	2.64
14	34	90	2.65
15	18	47	2.61

Table 11.2

Step 2: Calculate the $\bar{u}$ value.
The formula is:

$$\bar{u} = \frac{\text{Total number of defects}}{\text{Total inspection units}}$$

For our example, we inspected 376 units and found 863 defects. Our $\bar{u}$ value is $863 / 376 = 2.30$.

Step 3: Find the upper control limit for each sample.
The formula is:

$$UCL_u = \bar{u} + 3\sqrt{\bar{u}/n}$$

Step 4: Find the lower control limit for each sample.
The formula is:

$$LCL_u = \bar{u} - 3\sqrt{\bar{u}/n}$$

Table 11.3 shows the upper and lower control limits for our 15 samples.

Step 5: Set the scale, plot the data and draw the control limits on the chart.
Set the scale so the u-bar value is near the middle of the chart. For our sample the maximum scale would be about 4.80 and the minimum 0.

Figure 11.2 shows a u chart for our sample data.

Sample	UCL	LCL
1	3.10	1.49
2	3.43	1.16
3	3.20	1.39
4	3.34	1.25
5	3.56	1.03
6	3.02	1.57
7	3.15	1.44
8	3.11	1.48
9	3.43	1.16
10	3.29	1.30
11	3.05	1.54
12	3.24	1.35
13	3.20	1.39
14	3.07	1.52
15	3.37	1.22

Table 11.3

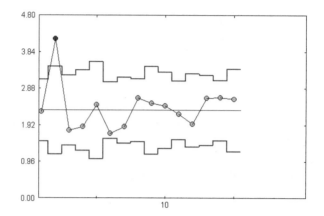

Figure 11.2
u chart from
our sample data

11.3 Demerit systems

Some defects are more serious than others and you may want to give
them more weight. For example, a defect that is surface or cosmetic
only is not as critical as one causing unit failure. One way to factor
in the seriousness of defects is to assign demerits to each defect type.
The more serious the defect, the higher the demerits.

For example, we'll give
minor surface defects
one demerit. For major
surface defects and
defects that might
cause unit failure, we'll
give two demerits. If
the defect definitely
causes unit failure,
we'll give it three
demerits. Now we'll
count defects by type
and plot the demerits

Defects on Finished Product

Part: __*RTG-098*__   Date: __*03-17-2001*__

Inspector: __*Patrick*__   Shift: __*3rd*__

Remarks: _____

Categories:

#1 Minor surface defects
i.e., surface scratches, small dents, small bubbles

~~THL~~ ~~THL~~ ~~THL~~ ~~THL~~ ~~THL~~ ~~THL~~
~~THL~~ ~~THL~~ /

Total: __*41*__

#2 Major surface defects/defects that might cause unit failure
i.e., uneven color, deep scratch, large bubbles dent, casing crack, loose
screw

~~THL~~ ~~THL~~ ~~THL~~
~~THL~~ //

Total: __*22*__   x 2 = __*44*__

#3 Defects that wil cause unit failure
i.e., loose wiring, improper wiring, missing screws

~~THL~~ ~~THL~~

Total: __*10*__   x 3 = __*30*__

Total units inspected this shift: __*120*__

Total demerits for this shift: __*115*__

Figure 11.3
Check sheet for
classifying defects by
their severity

instead of the defects. Figure 11.3 shows a sample check-sheet for a process using the demerit system.

11.4 Plotting defects by type

Both the u and c charts we've looked at showed us the total number of non-conformities for each sample. When we lump defects together, however, we can't detect trends in individual categories. One defect type may be increasing and another decreasing, but if we're only looking at the total defects, we won't see this. If there are only a few defect types, you might want to track them separately. Or you might want to track a few types of defects separately and group less common or less serious defects.

Obviously to track these defect types separately, we have to count them separately. One way to do this is to keep separate counts but plot samples based on the total count, as shown in Figure 11.4. You could also plot each type separately. For more detailed analysis, you may want to do both.

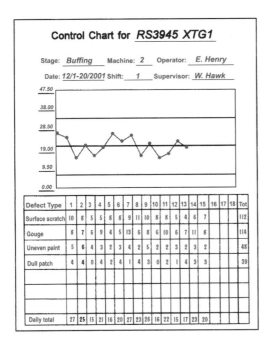

Figure 11.4
Control chart with tally of defects separated by type

12.0 Special charts for special applications

*It's hard to solve a problem when
you don't even know it exists.*

Fred Heiser

12.1 Short run SPC

Short run refers to processes that produce a high volume in a short time or a low volume over a long time. Processes producing one part per run or parts that are hard to subgroup are also short run. Because they produce fewer parts, they give us fewer samples to study. This creates a problem when we try to use conventional SPC, which is geared for high-volume, long-term processes. We can get around this by using control charts adapted for fewer samples.

Individual & Moving Range Charts
For some processes it isn't practical to use a sample size greater than one. The process may have a long cycle time such as a shift or day; the readings may be expensive, or they may be lengthy. An example of this is a reading from a destructive test.

In other cases, it may be unnecessary to use a sample size greater than one. Consider cases involving homogeneous chemical solutions such as taking pH readings from a swimming pool. No matter where you take the sample from the pool, it will be the same, so more than one sample is unnecessary. In both these examples, we base control charts on individual readings.

There are drawbacks to the individuals charts. They are easily misinterpreted if the distribution is non-normal. They aren't as sensitive to process changes as the X-bar & R, but they're overly sensitive to process variation. You may find yourself investigating more natural variation than you would with an X-bar & R chart. And with a sample size of one there is more variability in the average of samples ($\overline{X}$) until it is based on at least a hundred samples.

Like Median and X-bar charts, the control limits are based on sample range. With a sample size of one, there is no range, so we create a moving range, using two, three, or more readings. To find a moving range, find the range of the first reading and the second. This is the first range value. Then find the range between the second and third readings. This is the next range value and so on. If you use three readings, the first value is the range of the first, second and third readings, and the second value is the range of the second, third and fourth readings, etc.

Obs. No.	Reading	Mov. Range
1	10	—
2	12	2
3	15	3
4	18	3
5	12	6
6	11	1
7	13	2
8	14	1
9	18	4
10	17	1
11	12	5
12	14	2
13	13	1
14	11	2
15	18	7
16	16	2
17	15	1
18	17	2
19	13	4
20	11	2
	280	51

Table 12.1

To calculate the control limits for the moving range chart, use the average range for the center line, the $D_4 * \overline{R}$ formula for the upper control limit and zero for the lower control limit. The moving range size rarely exceeds five, so you would not need a D_3 factor for the lower control limit. (Appendix C has a table of these factors).

When you study this chart, keep in mind each reading appears in two ranges. Looking at every other range will give you independent ranges for conducting a run test.

For the Individuals chart we use a factor of 2.66 rather than A_2. For the center line we use the average of the samples. The $UCL_X = \overline{X} + (2.66 * \overline{R})$. The $LCL_X = \overline{X} + (2.66 * \overline{R})$. We set the chart scale for the Individuals & R chart as we would a X-bar & R chart.

If, for example, we have the 20 readings shown in the first column of Table 12.1, we would have the 19 ranges shown in the second column. The last row in this table shows the totals for each column.

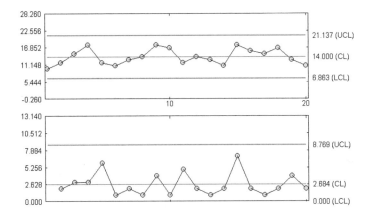

Figure 12.1
Individual & Moving Range Charts

Our X-bar would be calculated 280 / 20 = 14 and the R-bar would be 51 / 19 = 2.68.

The UCL_R would be 3.267 (D_4) * 2.68 = 8.76 and the LCL_R would equal zero. The UCL_x would be 14 + 7.13 = 21.13. The LCL_x for this sample is 14 – 7.13 = 6.87.

Figure 12.1 shows the individual and moving range charts from this data.

Moving Average Moving Range Charts
Moving Average Moving Range charts are also used for processes where it isn't practical to have a sample size greater than one. An example of this type of process is a continuous chemical process, where it isn't possible to sample small changes in consecutive parts.

Also like the Individuals chart, these charts are easy to misinterpret. This is because we repeat each reading in several samples. For example, with 22 readings we can create 20 samples of three. But, this isn't the same as having 20 samples from 60 readings.

We find the Moving Average the same way we find Moving Range. For a sample size of three, our first sample would be from readings

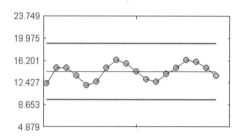

Figure 12.2
Moving average chart

1, 2, 3; the second from 2, 3, 4, etc. We calculate the control limits with the same formulas we use for an X-bar chart. Figure 12.2 shows a moving average chart made from the data we used for our individuals chart. In this example n=3, X-bar = 14.31, UCL = 18.98, and the LCL = 9.65.

Nominal Charts
Nominal charts let us plot data from different parts on one chart, using the same scale. For example, we would use this chart to plot data from short runs that produce several sizes of one part. To use this chart, all the parts must be from the same process and have similar standard deviations. The subgroup size must be constant for all samples and there must be a nominal value for each dimension.

To create a Nominal Chart:

Step 1: Set the nominal or target value for each part type.
The target value can be the required specification or the process average ($\overline{\overline{X}}$).

Step 2: Collect and record data and calculate subgroup averages.
This procedure is handled the same way as data for a conventional X-bar & R chart. For example, let's look at three bolt runs; the first produces a 2" bolt, the second a 3" bolt and the third a 5" bolt. We want to monitor the length of the bolts in each run. The data and its averages for our example are shown in Table 12.2.

Step 3: Code the subgroup averages.
The formula is:

$$c = a - t$$

where c = the coded value,
a = subgroup average and
t = target value.

The target value for our 2" bolt is 2, for the 3" bolt is 3, and for the 5" is 4. Table 12.3 shows the coded value for each subgroup.

Step 4 : Find the range for each subgroup.

The range for the nominal chart is the same as the range for the conventional X-bar & R chart. R = the highest value – the lowest.

Table 12.4 shows the ranges for our samples.

Step 5: Find the control limits for the Range chart.

These limits use the same formulas as the Range chart for conventional SPC. These formulas are:

$$\overline{R} = \frac{\Sigma R}{k}$$

2"	m1	m2	m3	Avg.
1	2.08	2.05	2.12	2.08
2	2.00	2.10	2.07	2.06
3	1.95	2.01	2.03	2.00
4	1.93	1.96	2.02	1.97
5	2.11	2.14	2.05	2.10

3"	m1	m2	m3	Avg.
1	3.02	3.08	3.10	3.07
2	3.00	2.95	2.97	2.97
3	3.10	3.13	3.08	3.10
4	3.07	3.02	2.98	3.02
5	3.04	3.12	3.09	3.08

5"	m1	m2	m3	Avg.
1	5.0	5.07	4.99	5.02
2	5.10	5.15	5.08	5.11
3	5.02	5.03	5.07	5.04
4	5.02	4.92	4.94	4.96
5	5.10	5.04	5.06	5.07

Table 12.2

2"	Avg.	Code	3"	Avg.	Code	5"	Avg.	Code
1	2.08	0.08	1	3.07	0.07	1	5.02	0.02
2	2.06	0.06	2	2.97	-0.03	2	5.11	0.11
3	2.00	0.00	3	3.10	0.10	3	5.04	0.04
4	1.97	-0.03	4	3.02	0.02	4	4.96	-0.04
5	2.10	0.10	5	3.08	0.08	5	5.07	0.07

Table 12.3

2"	R	3"	R	5"	R
1	0.07	1	0.08	1	0.08
2	0.10	2	0.05	2	0.07
3	0.08	3	0.05	3	0.05
4	0.09	4	0.09	4	0.10
5	0.09	5	0.08	5	0.06

Table 12.4

$$UCL = D_4 * \overline{R}$$

$$LCL = D_3 * \overline{R}$$

A table of the D_3 and D_4 factors appears in Appendix C.

For our example the $\overline{R}$ = 1.11 / 15 = 0.074. The UCL = 2.575 * 0.074 = 0.191 and the LCL = 0.00.

Step 6: Calculate the control limits for the Nominal chart.
Use the coded values for these calculations. The formulas for this are the same as for a conventional X-bar chart.

$$\overline{\overline{X}} = \frac{\Sigma \overline{X}}{k}$$

$$UCL = \overline{\overline{X}} + (A_2 * \overline{R})$$

$$LCL = \overline{\overline{X}} - (A_2 * \overline{R})$$

For a complete Table of Factors, see Appendix C.

For our example, the $\overline{\overline{X}}$ = 0.65 / 15 = 0.043. The UCL = (1.023 * 0.074) + 0.043 = 0.119. The LCL = 0.043 – 0.076 = –0.033.

Step 7: Set the scale and plot the codes and ranges on the control charts.

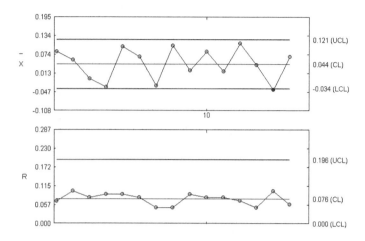

Figure 12.3
Nominal & Range chart

Again, this follows the same rule as the conventional X-bar & R. Subtract the lower control limit from the upper control limit and divide this value by two. Add this to the upper control limit for the maximum scale and subtract it from the lower control limit for the minimum scale.

For our Range chart, the upper scale value = 0.191 / 2 = 0.286 and since range can't be less than zero, the lower scale value is 0.00.

For our Nominal chart, the upper scale value = 0.119 − (−0.032) = 0.151 / 2 = 0.195. The lower scale value = −0.032 − 0.076 = −0.108.

Figure 12.3 shows a Nominal X-bar & Range chart for our data.

Interpret the Nominal chart the same way you interpret a conventional X-bar & R chart For more information, review Chapter 8.0, *Control Chart Analysis*.

12.2 Toolwear charts

As discussed in Chapter 1, control charts help us predict the behavior of a stable process and compare our current readings to that prediction. Until now, we've thought of a stable process as one in which the samples fall between the control limits, showing no change in the process. However, there are cases where a process has a constant, predictable change, such as that caused by toolwear. When tool wear affects a process, the control chart will show cycles. Each tool change or adjustment starts a new cycle, which shows a gradual shift in sample averages as the tool wears down. These cycles make it necessary to adjust control limits so they reflect the predicted change. This adjustment is pictured in Figure 12.4. The upper chart is an X-bar chart for a process of this type. We can see more variance between the sample averages than the limits predicted. The result is out of control signals from variation that we expect the process to have. In the lower chart, a toolwear chart, the limits reflect the process cycles. Any out-of-control points here would have a special cause. In addition to filtering our expected variation, a toolwear chart lets us pinpoint when tool adjustments or replacements need to be made.

To adjust the control limits, we must find the slope (m), intercept (c), and control limits for each cycle.

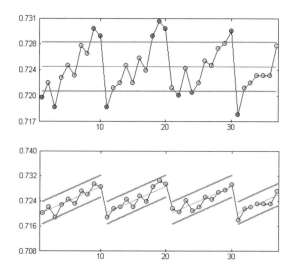

Figure 12.4
The upper chart
showing a regular
X-bar chart of our data
with a linear trend.
The lower chart is a
toolwear chart of the
same data.

x	x²	y	xy	R
1	1	1.5500	1.55000	0.25
2	4	1.6067	3.21340	0.20
3	9	1.6567	4.97010	0.25
4	16	1.7000	6.80000	0.20
5	25	1.7533	8.76650	0.17
6	36	1.7900	10.7400	0.20
7	49	1.8500	12.9500	0.08
28	784	11.9067	48.9900	1.35
				0.19286

Table 12.5

Step 1: Begin by creating a table as shown in Table 12.5

You need to know the values of x, x^2, y and xy, and the sums of these. In this case x = the subgroup's number and y = the subgroup's average. You'll also need the range for the range chart and the toolwear chart's control limits.

Step 2: Create a range chart.

The range chart that accompanies the toolwear chart is the same as the range chart for an X-bar chart.

Step 3: Calculate the slope and intercept of the toolwear chart's center line.

The formula for the slope is:

$$m = \frac{\Sigma(xy) - \dfrac{(\Sigma x)(\Sigma y)}{n}}{\Sigma(x^2) - \dfrac{(\Sigma x)^2}{n}}$$

The formula for the intercept (c) is:

$$c = \frac{(\Sigma x)\, (\Sigma xy) - (\Sigma y)\, (\Sigma x^2)}{(\Sigma x)^2 - n\, (\Sigma x^2)}$$

Using the data from Table 12.5:

$$m = \frac{48.99 - \dfrac{(28 * 11.9067)}{7}}{140 - \dfrac{28^2}{7}} = 0.04869$$

$$c = \frac{(28 * 48.99) - (119067 * 140)}{28^2 - (7 * 140)} = 1.5062$$

Step 4: Use the slope and intercept to find the center line.
The formula for the center line is:

$$\bar{\bar{y}} = mx + c$$

Although you can calculate a y value for each sample, you only need to do this for the first and last samples in the cycle. Then draw a straight line to connect them.

If we use the samples from our example:

First point: $(0.04869 * 1) + 1.5062 = 1.55489$

Last point: $(0.04869 * 7) + 1.5062 = 1.84703$

Step 5: Find the control limits.
The control limits here use the same formula as the control limits for a regular X-bar chart. However, for the toolwear chart, the upper control limit is the last point above the center line $+ (A_2 * R)$. Likewise, the lower control limits is the first point above the center line $- (A_2 * R)$. To draw the control limits, $(A_2 * R) = 0.1973$.

Using our example:

$$UCL_1 = 1.55489 + 0.1973 = 1.75219$$
$$LCL_1 = 1.84703 + 0.1973 = 2.04433$$

$$UCL_7 = 1.55489 - 0.1973 = 1.35759$$
$$LCL_7 = 1.84703 - 0.1973 = 1.64973$$

Step 6: Set the chart's scale.
Subtract the LCL from the UCL and divide this difference by two. Add this value to the largest UCL value for the chart's maximum value. Subtract it from the smallest LCL value for the chart's minimum value.

For our example, the maximum scale value is:

$$2.04433 - 1.35797 = 0.686733 / 2 = 0.3433665$$

$$2.04433 + 0.34337 = 2.3877$$

The minimum is:

$$1.35797 - 0.34337 = 1.0146$$

Step 7: Plot the data points and the control limit points and connect them.
As with the X-bar chart, points falling outside the control limits indicate a change in the process.

The lengthy calculations needed for a toolwear chart can be tedious and time-consuming when done by hand. Fortunately, we can use computers to do the math and draw the limits quickly, so the toolwear chart is just as easy to access as a regular control chart.

12.3 Three Charts

We use X-bar charts to study the variation between samples and Range charts to see the variation within a sample. Usually, these charts give us the data we need to control our process. However, if we batch process our products or produce rolled goods, we also need to look at batch-to-batch variation. For example, if we're producing sheet metal, we'll want to know the variation between the machine direction and the cross direction. To do this, we need to combine a Moving Range chart with a our X-bar & R chart. This combination is called a Three chart or a Three-Way chart.

To create a Three Chart:

Step 1: Collect and record data.
In order to use this chart, we need collect several readings from each batch.

Step 2: Create an X-bar & R chart from sample data.
This is a conventional X-bar and R chart as described in Chapter 6.

Step 3:   Calculate the Moving Range (Rm).
To do this, find the range of the first and second sample averages, the second and third sample averages, the third and fourth sample averages, etc. Table 12.6 shows moving ranges for the 20 samples we used in Chapter 6.

Sample	1	2	3	4	5	6	7	8	9	10
Range	0.30	0.30	0.29	0.65	0.50	0.30	0.30	0.79	0.39	0.35
Mov. Range	—	0.40	0.05	0.01	0.03	0.31	0.40	0.11	0.05	0.17

Sample	11	12	13	14	15	16	17	18	19	20
Range	0.30	0.30	0.54	0.23	0.30	0.53	0.79	0.74	0.39	0.20
Mov. Range	0.18	0.40	0.06	0.11	0.17	0.26	0.15	0.03	0.08	0.09

Table 12.6

Step 4: Calculate the control limits and plot the data.
The Moving Range chart uses the same formula as a conventional Range chart. The $\overline{R}$ = the average of the moving ranges.

The UCL = $D_4 * \overline{R}$ and the LCL = $D_3 * \overline{R}$.
For our example:

$\overline{R}$ = 3.07 / 19 = 0.16157

UCL = 3.267 * 0.16157 = 0.52784 and the LCL = 0.

Figure 12.5 shows a Three Chart of our data.

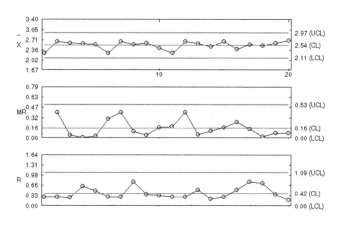

Figure 12.5
Three chart

13.0 Getting started

Many things which cannot be overcome when they are together,
yield themselves up when taken little by little.

Plutarch

Starting an SPC program is not easy. There is no magic formula, no blueprint, no machine that makes it happen. Starting an SPC program means changing the way you do business, changing the way you think about business. It takes a commitment from everyone in the company, top down, to make it work. It takes education and teamwork. A successful SPC program throws aside the "us vs. them" attitude between management and workers, in favor of working as a team for the good of all. These changes will not happen ovemight.

While there is no blueprint for starting your program, successful SPC programs share the same basic parts. First and foremost is education.

13.1 Education

To make your SPC program a success, your company must be educated about SPC concepts. Show employees what SPC can do for your company. You may have to sell them on the concepts of continuous improvement and process control, as well as teach them how SPC works. Teach them to focus on the process and not the outputs.

One place to begin is with a study of your production process and the costs of poor quality. Look at the amount of scrap and rework, what it costs to replace or repair poor quality, and the cost of additional labor incurred. Consider how much time is spent resolving customer complaints. Have you lost customers because of poor quality? Factor this in as well.

Then, look at how much your company could save by controlling your process. Controlling your process means preventing problems instead of fixing them. Eliminating non-conformities means you'll save money. Instead of repairing defects, your employees can redeploy their efforts, so you'll see an increase in productivity. Better quality also helps create customer loyalty. Look at how SPC can improve your process and your bottom line.

Whom do you educate? Start with the top. Your program won't succeed unless you have the support of top management. You'll have to show why the company needs SPC. For this group, focus on benefits, measurable results, savings and contributions to the corporate bottom line. They'll also need to understand SPC techniques well enough to have faith in the results and invest in its success. In many cases, the implementation cost will be recouped quickly—often in as little as a few months or even weeks. Management must spend the time to thoroughly understand SPC theories and charting. After all, some very important business decisions will be made from chart information.

Next, educate engineering and quality control people. These groups are likely to spearhead the initial efforts and should be trained as "internal" consultants that can help identify and resolve problems.

Finally, operators and production supervisors must understand what the charts are for and what they show. They must be trained to read charts and to act to correct the process when the charts show it is necessary.

13.2 Making the transition to SPC

Don't expect everyone to jump on the SPC bandwagon at once. Some people are intimidated by statistics. In the beginning, when people are learning process control, there will be additional tasks involved. Some people will undoubtedly complain about the extra work of charting. As people learn and apply SPC methods, preventing problems will gradually replace fixing them.

Management should keep an eye on the transition to SPC. Old ways die hard, so be patient and persistent. Problems often occur at this stage because people feel they lack the skills needed to do the work. If more training is needed, provide it.

To help smooth the transition process, there must be someone workers can go to with questions or to mediate disputes over chart information. This is where your internal consultants come in. Control charts are easy to make, but sometimes interpreting them is difficult. It may take time for workers to feel comfortable with their decisions to act or not act. But there is no substitute for experience.

13.3 The Production Worker's role in SPC

Production workers are vital to the success of the program, because they have the best view of the process. Only production workers know firsthand the current practices and problems on the floor. Chances are they have a good sense of their equipment's capabilities and how to tweak it to make it do what they want. They can take or at least suggest corrective action; therefore, problem solving must include their input.

Without their input, process improvements are likely to be short lived. If they don't agree with the proposed solution, they may simply 'forget' to do it that way. If they've helped come up with a solution, they'll want to see it work.

13.4 Management's role

As mentioned, management must have faith in SPC methods. Managers must respond to chart data and encourage production workers to do the same.

How important is management to the success of the program? One company began an SPC program in its four departments, giving each the same training. Two of them reported great success, cutting waste and improving productivity. In the other two, the program had no effect. In fact, productivity had decreased.

An investigation showed supervisors and management in the successful departments responded to the indications on the charts. They encouraged workers to make changes and monitored the effects with the charts.

The other departments made, but ignored the charts. No changes were made to operating practices. Workers had to keep the charts, but nothing came of their efforts. They complained about doing extra work for nothing.

13.5 Start slowly

Most companies with successful SPC programs didn't try to convert all their processes at once, they selected one target area. What problem is the most costly? What problem seems to have a high probability of success? Pareto analysis can help you decide what to tackle first.

Once you've targeted a problem, determine what key characteristics should be measured. Again you should start small. Identify a couple characteristics, and save the rest until you expand your program. Then determine how data will be collected and recorded. How will you take measurements? What sample size will you use?

Gather data, create your control chart, and calculate control limits. Base your limits on at least 20 samples. Study the chart. Is data out of control or are there definite trends? Work on removing special causes of variation. Find and correct assignable causes. Gather more data, plot and analyze it. Did the changes improve your process or make it worse? React to your findings. Study the capability of the process. Is it capable of producing the output you require?

13.6 The next step

Continue the cycle of gathering data, plotting it, studying it, and reacting to it. When you are comfortable with the process of process control, expand to include related characteristics. When you are comfortable with those, add others or bring a new target area into focus. Keep adding new areas until everything is under control. Once everything is up and running, keep working to improve the product.

It's easy to get discouraged, especially if your process adjustments do the opposite of what you expect them to. Sometimes you'll have setbacks. Making the gradual shift to SPC allows you and your co-workers to become more familar with SPC techniques and how they apply to your company. It allows you to pinpoint areas that need more training or better equipment. But most importantly, it keeps you from getting overwhelmed.

14.0 Automating SPC

Data are most valuable at their point of origin.
The value of data is directly related to their timeliness.

Lawrence M. Miller

Unless you skipped from page one to this chapter, you know how to create SPC charts. You also know performing calculations and drawing charts by hand is very time-consuming. If you let a computer do the work, however, you can have up-to-date SPC charts instantaneously.

This instant access to process data means you know exactly when a process is out of control and can adjust it before precious time and materials go to waste. So while you'll have to spend money to automate your SPC program, you'll get it back quickly by reducing scrap and labor costs.

14.1 Automating data entry

In Chapter 9, we looked at measurement error and how digital gages reduce variance. These devices feed data directly into computers, which helps reduce data entry errors. Operators simply measure a part, press a button on the device, and the data is saved to the system.

The device you buy depends on what you want to measure, as well as your SPC system. There are devices for measuring size, weight, temperature, color, etc. Some of these work with a specific SPC system, others are more flexible. Depending on the device and your needs, you may be able to link one device to each computer or route several of them to one computer.

14.2 Automating charts and calculations

With automated SPC, data enters the system and immediately appears on the control chart. The computer finds the average, ranges or sigma and instantly the results of a sample is drawn on the chart. It calculates control limits and alerts you to out-of-control conditions. Once the data is in the system you can view it in control charts and histograms or perform capability studies.

Some systems let you enter data into several files at once and view charts for each on one screen. There are network-based systems, which send data from a number of workstations into one or more files. The most sophisticated SPC implementations support enterprise-wide quality management with an integrated view of every process in real time across multiple network sites. Using their desktop PC as a "command central" for quality, an executive can monitor the precise status of all production activity regardless of location. Color-coded alarms alert the user to out-of-control or out-of-specification conditions and incoming messages. Interactive features allow you to zoom in on a single characteristic for details about that process. Enterprise-wide systems also provide extensive global process reporting capabilities.

14.3 Hardware-dependent vs. flexible systems

Automated SPC programs fall into two categories: hardware-dependent and flexible. With hardware-dependent systems, the gages, computer and software are made by one company. This software only runs on this proprietary computer and only accepts data from these gages. Implementing this type of system limits the number of vendors you have to deal with; however, updating it may mean you have to replace the entire system every time.

Flexible systems are software-based and work with a combination of hardware. They accept data from any standard measuring device, run on standard Windows®-based computers, and print to a variety of printers. The software is independent of the hardware, and usually comes from another company. This system is ideal if you want to use computers you already have and lets you run other software, such as spreadsheets word processors and e-mail programs, on the same computer so you won't need a dedicated machine.

Personal Data Assistants (PDAs) now offer a cost-effective option for organizations that want to incorporate portable data collection into their SPC activities. These units accept data from the shop floor and upload a measurement process to a host computer for data ware-housing, analysis or reporting using an interface to a full-fledged SPC software package.

Recent innovations in wireless network technology allow works to move freely about the production facility and perform SPC without being physically connected to the network. Wireless SPC computers provide the security of data storage on the network server, eliminating the possibility of losing data if the wireless device is misplaced or broken. These mobile units range in function from dedicated units that only perform data collection and barebones charting on miniature LCD screens to the latest pen tablet units that are fully functional PCs for statistical process control as well as running other software applications, accessing files stored on the network server or sending and receiving e-mail (Figure 14.1).

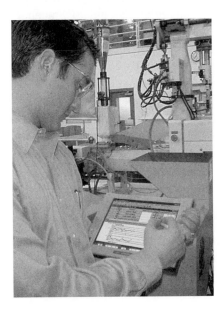

Figure 14.1
A wireless pen tablet being used for SPC

14.4 Choosing a system

Before deciding on an SPC system, look at your application. What variables will you measure? How do you want to enter data? If you're looking at diverse variables that required different gages, you'll probably want a flexible system. A Quality Engineer or Process Engineer may want to design control charts, analyze out-of-control data points or extract information about a process off line. In that case, a statistical analysis software package can provide additional capabilities that fall outside the realm of traditional SPC software.

Will you need or want to update your system at some point? If you foresee little change in your SPC program, a hardware-dependent system might be what you need. But keep in mind that computer and SPC technology change all the time, so these systems often become obsolete in a few years. Flexible programs are usually easier and less expensive to update because you don't have to change the entire system at once.

Make sure your Information Technology Department is represented in the decision process. They will want reassurance on system compatibility, networking requirements, data portability and how much (or how little) technical support they will be expected to provide.

Look at the flexible programs carefully. Some let you use any computer but lock you into a few gages. Others update their software and change the file format, so you have to redo all of your old work. Still others never change. The ideal system adds and improves features regularly to take advantage of new SPC applications and technology, as well as new computer technology. At the same time, it keeps the system compatible with the old files. Avoid software programs that require on-going IT programming resources every time you want to create a report. That defeats the reason that you automated your SPC activities in the first place. You may also want to consider a system that lets you start with basic SPC functions and add more elaborate features as your quality program develops.

14.5 Bringing your program on-line

Bringing your SPC system on-line is the same as starting a new program. Begin by learning the system and training your employees. Those with no computer experience will need to learn the basics as well as the software and data entry methods. When you are ready to go live, start with one process, so you and your employees aren't overwhelmed. When that process is up to stable and capable, gradually add new ones, until everything is on line.

References/Bibliography

AT&T Corporation. *Statistical Quality Control Handbook.* 2nd ed. Charlotte: Delmar Printing Co., 1985.

Automotive Industry Action Group. *Measurement Systems Analysis.* 2nd ed. Detroit: 1995.

Automotive Industry Action Group. *Fundamental Statistical Process Control.* 2nd ed. Detroit: 1995.

Bothe, Davis R. *Measuring Process Capability: Techniques and Calculations for Quality and Manufacturing Engineeers.* New York: McGraw-Hill, 1997.

Duncan, Acheson J. *Quality Control and Industrial Statistics.* 5th ed. Chicago: Richard D. Irwin Inc., 1986.

Decker, David. "An Explanation of ISO 9000." Emporia State U. 27 Mar. 2002 <http: academic. emporia.edu/smithwil/598mgt423/eJAwebs/decker.htm>.

Grant, Eugene, and Richard Leavenworth. *Statistical Quality Control.* 7th ed. New York: McGraw-Hill, 1996.

The IBM Quality Institute. *Process Control, Capability and Improvement.* New York: 1984.

Koval, Harry H. "Are You Using the Right SPC Charts and Limits? or 'My Gosh, Is My Process Out of Control?'" Presentation. 3M, St. Paul: 1996.

Manugistics, Inc. "Integrating Statgraphics Plus into a Six Sigma Program." August 1999.

Pyzdek, Thomas. "In Defense of Six Sigma: What it is, and what it isn't." *Quality Digest* March 2002: 64.

Ryan, Thomas P. *Statistical Methods for Quality Improvement.* 2nd ed. New York: John Wiley & Sons, Inc., 2000.

"Six-Sigma Design." U of Virginia. 13 Dec. 1998. <http://www.people.virginia.edu/~shj2n/design/1design6. html>.

Waxer, Charles. "Six Sigma Organizational Architecture." 23 Apr. 2002. <http://www.isixsigma.com/library/content/C010128a.asp>.

Common Symbols

χ^2	Chi-square
k	The number of samples in a study
μ	Mean
n	The number of readings in one sample. For example: $n = 3$ means the sample has three readings.
N	The total number of readings in a study
R	The range of a sample
$\bar{R}$	The average range
$\tilde{R}$	The median of a range
s	The standard deviation of a sample
$\bar{s}$	The average of the standard deviation
σ	The standard deviation of an entire population
σ^2	Variance
Σ	Used in formulas as the command "sum"
X	A random variable
x_i	Refers to a specific reading, but not the exact value. For example: x_1, x_5, x_3.
$\bar{X}$	The sample average
$\bar{\bar{X}}$	The average of the sample averages
$\tilde{X}$	The median of a sample
$\tilde{\tilde{X}}$	The median of the sample medians

Glossary

Accuracy	How close the measured value is to the true value
Assignable cause	See *Special cause*
Attribute	Data that can be counted, such as go/no-go or the number of defects.
Attribute charts	Charts used to plot attribute data: c, np, p and u charts
Automated SPC	Computerized statistical process control where the computer performs calculations and plots data on the control chart. This concept includes direct data input.
Average	The sum of a group of values divided by the number of values in the group; also known as *mean*
Bell-shaped curve	The shape of a normal distribution, so-called because it has a peak in the middle and tapers off on either side
Bias	A sampling error that distorts the average of a population. For example, selecting only items with visible defects would create a biased statistic of the population.
Binomial distribution	A probability distribution for attribute data when only two outcomes are possible, such as pass/fail or go/no-go
Brainstorming	A problem-solving method in which group members first generate a number of possible solutions and then discuss their merits

Bunching	A distribution pattern where a group of samples have the same or similar readings. It indicates a sudden change in the cause of variation.
c chart	A control chart for attribute data used to plot the number of non-conformities in a fixed-size sample
Capability	The ability of a process to produce output within specification limits
Cause & effect diagram	A problem-solving tool used to analyzesources of process variation. Also called an *Ishikawa diagram* or a *fishbone diagram.*
Center line	On a control chart, the horizontal line in the center of the chart which represents the average or median of the process
Central Limit Theorem	Law of distribution that states no matter what the shape of the distribution of the universe, the distribution of the sample averages will move toward a normal distribution as the sample size increases
Central tendency	A measuredescribing the middle of a distribution. Four ways to measure central tendency are *midrange, median, mode* and *mean* (or average)
Characteristic	A feature of a part or its process, such as its dimensions, speed, hardness, temperature, smoothness, flatness, elasticity or weight
Check sheet	A form for recording data. Check sheets are designed for the specific type of data that is collected. For example, there are check sheets for measured data, for defects, for causes, for location, and for distribution. They usually include spaces to record the study date, time, method of collecting data, where the data comes from, and who collected it
Chi-square test	Shows how well the actual distribution fits the expected distribution, and is used to determine the likelihood of a distribution

Common causes	Sources of variation that are inherent in a process. These are random or chance causes.
Continuous improvement	Constantly making processes and products better to stay competitive
Control	The state of a process where no special or assignable causes of variation are present. Also called *statistical control.*
Control chart	A graph used to track a process to determine if the process is in control and if it is staying in control
Control limit	Control chart boundaries for a process in control which allow for common cause variation. When data falls outside these limits, it is out of control and signals a change in the process.
Cost of quality	The price of nonconformance (costs of not conforming to requirements) and the price of conformance (costs of procedure compliance); used within an organization to improve quality and increase profitability.
Cp	A capability index that reflects how well the process satisfies the specification
Cpk	A capability index used to measure process centering
Customer	Those who receive the output of a process. The customer may be the next step in the overall process or the person buying the end product.
Cycles	A recurring pattern on a control chart which signals something is changing over time
Data	Facts, usually numerical, about a process. SPC has two types of data, variable or attribute, which can be further classified by their purpose, such as analysis, process control or acceptance
Detection	A quality control procedure that identifies unacceptable products after production is complete instead of preventing their occurrence

Dispersion	The spread of values around the cental tendency of the process
Distribution	A way of describing the behavior of process data using the shape, dispersion and location of the data
Engineering tolerance	Process specifications for judging the quality of a product
Feedback	Data on the output of the process which is given to those involved so they can make necessary adjustments
Flexible SPC system	SPC software that is compatible with a wide variety of computer hardware
Freaks	A pattern where a single point periodically falls outside control limits
Gage acceptability	A value used to compare a gage's capability to the specification limits
Hardware-dependent SPC system	A system that only operates on a specific brand of computer or hardware
Histogram	A graph used to illustrate how often values occur. They also show how the data distribution relates to the spec limits, the share of the distribution, the central values and the dispersion.
Individual	A single reading; individuals are plotted when readings are difficult or expensive to obtain.
Individual & moving range	Control chart combination where one chart plots individual readings and the second chart plots moving range
Instability	Describes a process that is not in control. Usually shows unnaturally large fluctuations with points outside control limits on both sides of the center line.
Ishikawa diagram	See *Cause & Effect Diagram*

Kurtosis	The degree of flatness of a curve. See *platykurtic* and *leptokurtic*.
Lean manufacturing	A philosophy of producing only the product needed at the time it is needed using minimal resources such as labor, floor space, time and materials; also called *just-in-time manufacturing* or *JIT*.
Leptokurtic	A curve which is higher than the normal curve and has a kurtosis value that is less than zero
Lower control limit (LCL)	The lower boundary for a process which is in control
Lower specification (LSL)	The lowest acceptable dimension or value of *limit* a part or process
Manufacturing quality	How well the product meets the design
Mean	The average of a group of values
Mean Absolute Deviation (MAD)	A measure of dispersion which is the average distance from the center value
Measurement error	The difference between a measured value and the actual value
Median	The middle value of a group of data that has been sorted in ascending or descending order
Median chart	A control chart in which the median of each sample is plotted and the center line is the median of the sample medians
Mid-range	The midpoint of a range
Mixtures	A pattern reflecting two separate populations plotted on one chart. This often shows points alternating above and below the center line.
Mode	The value that occurs most frequently in a sample

Moving average	Average created by creating rational subgroups of samples; for example: samples 1&2, 2&3, 3&4.
Moving average moving range chart	A control chart used when it isn't practical to have a sample size greater than one
Moving range	Range created by creating rational subgroups of samples; for example: samples 1,2&3; 2,3&4; 3,4&5
Natural tolerance	The natural operating range of the process. Control limits form the boundaries for this tolerance.
Nominal	The target value
Nominals chart	A control chart used in short-run SPC that lets us plot data representing different parts on one chart. Data points are based on their relation to the nominal value. The parts must be from the same process and have similar standard deviations, have the same sample size, but they can be different sizes. For example: screws of the same style but different lengths.
Non-conforming unit	A part or product that's rejected because of one or more defects
Non-conformities	A flaw or blemish on a product which may or may not cause it to be rejected. See *Defect*.
Normal curve	A bell-shaped curve representing a normal distribution of data. See *Normal Distribution*.
Normal distribution	A symmetrical distribution of data where the likelihood of an event occurring increases as the values move toward the center or mean value and tail off again as they move beyond the center. The mean, median and mode are equal. In a normal distribution, 68.26% of the data fall with in 1σ on either side of the mean, 95.44% within 2σ and 99.73% within 3σ.
np chart	An attribute chart used to plot the number of non-conforming units when the sample size is equal. See *p chart*.

Observation	An individual measurement which is usually grouped to create a sample
Operator variability	Measurement variance caused by human interpretation of the process, gage, etc.
Out-of-control	A process that has variation exceeding the control limits. On control charts, it is reflected by samples outside the control limits.
Out-of-spec	Products that don't meet customer or engineering specification limits
p chart	An attribute chart used to plot the number of non-conforming units when the sample size varies. This chart uses a fraction based on the number of non-conforming units and the total number of units inspected. See *np chart*.
Pareto analysis	A technique used to prioritize problems. It's based on Vilfredo Pareto's economic theory of the vital few and the trivial many, where a few problems cause the most damage and the majority of the problems do the rest. Its goal is to identify which are the "vital few" problems that should be tackled first.
Pareto chart	The chart used in Pareto analysis, which combines a bar chart and a line plot to show which causes occur most often and at what cost.
Pattern	A design appearing in the control chart when the process is not behaving randomly. See *cycles, trends, mixtures, stratification, shifts, instability, bunching and freaks*.
Performance quality	The measure of a product's dependability. This type of quality is affected by how often a product fails, the time between failures, the time needed to repair it, and the repair costs.
Platykurtic	A curve that is flatter than a normal curve and has a kurtosis value greater than zero.

Poisson Distribution	A distribution that occurs when the probability that a specific event will occur is the same and the number of trials is large. It gets its name from Simeon Poisson, who first described it.
Population	In statistics, this is the entire group of items in a study. It can be people, screws, all parts made by one machine, etc. In SPC we study samples taken from the population to learn about its features. Also called *universe*.
Precision	Refers to how readings spread out around the average value.
Prevention	A method of quality control that emphasizes preventing quality problems from occurring during the production process instead of detecting and correcting them after production.
Probability	The chance that something will happen. Probability is a statistical estimate of the odds that an event will occur and how often.
Process	The entire system of machines, raw materials, people, procedures, environment and measurements used to make a product or service.
Process average	The average of sample averages in a process. This creates the center line on a control chart. Also called Xdouble bar ($\overline{\overline{X}}$).
Quality	With manufactured products and services, quality determined by the customer who judges quality by considering if the product does what is expected, competitive products, cost and personal preference. See *Design quality, Manufacturing quality and Performance quality*.
Quality control	A system for checking and maintaining the desired level of quality through design, process monitoring and reacting to process changes.
R chart	See *Range chart*

Random sample	A sample in which any part of the population has an equal chance of being selected
Range	The difference between the highest and lowest values in a sample. Used to study variation between readings in a sample.
Range chart	A control chart for variable data used to plot the sample ranges. Also called *R chart*.
Reading	An individual measurement. Also called *observation*.
Repeatability	Equipment variation found when one person measures the same dimension several times with the same gage
Reproducibility	Variation found between operators when two or more people measure the same dimension with the same gage
Run	A group of points on one side of the center line.
Run chart	A control chart where individual readings are plotted in chronological order so that runs can be detected
s chart	See *Sigma chart*
Sample	A subgroup of readings used to represent a population
Sample average	The average value of the readings in a subgroup
Sample range	The range of the readings in a subgroup
Sample size	The number of readings in a subgroup
Sampling	The process of collecting readings for a sample
Sampling plan	A plan for collecting random samples that accurately represent the population. Sampling plans include how samples will be collected, how often they'll be taken and the sample size

Scatter diagram	A chart used to determine the relationship between a cause and effect or between two causes. One axis represents one cause and the second axis represents the other cause or effect.
Sensitivity	The degree to which control charts reflect process variation. A more sensitive chart may show even slight natural varation as an out-of-control process, while a less sensitive chart may show excessive variation as "in control."
Shewhart Control Chart	See *Control chart*
Shifts	A sudden change in a pattern such as a jump or drop. It can indicate a change in operators or raw materials or a shift in process operations.
Short-run SPC	SPC techniques used for process that produce a high volume in a short time or a low volume over a long time. It also applies to those producing one part per run or parts that are hard to subgroup. Charts used for short-run SPC include Individual & Moving Range, Moving Average & Moving Range, Nominal Charts and Standardized charts.
Sigma	The standard deviation of a population.
Sigma chart	The control chart for variable data plots standard deviations of samples. Also called s chart. Note that σ is the standard deviation of the sample and σ represents the standard deviation of the population. *These are not the same thing!*
Six Sigma	An approach to quality pioneered in the 1980s by Motorola that maintains that average processes operate at a three-sigma level; best-in-class at six sigma. The approach is based on the fundamental that companies subscribing to six sigma experience only 3.4 defects per million opportunities.
Skew	The difference between the mean and the mode. The skew factor shows if the process leans toward the upper or lower specifications.

Special cause	Sources of variation which are identifiable such as human error or equipment failure. These interfere with the process causing an irregular output.
Specification	The engineering requirements used to judge the quality of a product. Specifications are often based on customer requirements.
Spread	See *Dispersion*
Stability	A process that is in statistical control. Variation is limited and falls within control limits.
Standard deviation	A measure of process spread which squares the difference between a value and the average, divides it by the number of values, and takes the square root of that value.
Statistic	A calculated value derived from the sample data. Statistics are estimates of the true population values.
Statistical control	A process with no special or assignable causes of variation.
Statistical process control	The practice of using statistics to detect variations in a process so they can be controlled, thereby controlling the quality of the output.
Stratification	A control chart pattern where data points appear to hug the center line, with points alternating on either side of it.
Subgroup	See *Sample*
Three chart	A control chart group used to look at batch-to-batch variation as well as variation between samples and within a sample. Three charts combine X-bar & R charts with a Moving Range chart.
Tolerance	See *Specification, Engineering Tolerances* and *Natural Tolerances*.

Toolwear charts	A modified control chart used to compensate for expected variation caused by toolwear and replacement.
Trend	A control chart pattern that shows constant change, such as that caused by toolwear.
Trial control limits	Control limits based on the first 20-25 samples, which are used to determine if the process is in control.
u chart	A control chart for attribute data used to plot the number of non-conformities when the sample size varies. This chart uses a fraction based on the number of defects in the sample and the number of units in the sample. See *c chart*.
Uniform distribution	A distribution that occurs when each possible outcome has an equal chance of occurring; also called *rectangular distribution*.
Universe	See *population*
Upper Control Limit (UCL)	The upper boundary for a process that is in control
Upper Specification Limit (USL)	The largest acceptable dimension or value of a part or process
Variable	Data that can be measured such as length, weight, speed, temperature or diameter
Variable charts	Charts used to plot variable data such as X-bar & R and s charts.
Variance	A measure of spread which is the standard deviation squared; see *standard deviation*.
Variation	The difference between outputs of the same process. Sometimes it is a natural part of the process, but other times, it has a special cause which should be eliminated.

X-bar chart   A control chart for variable data which plots the sample averages. Is used to study variation between samples.

X-bar & s chart   A control chart combination of the X-bar and sigma chart

Z-score   A statistic used to estimate how much of a product falls outside specification limits

Appendices

Appendix A

SPC Formulae

p chart

$$\bar{p} = \frac{\text{Total number of non-conforming units}}{\text{Total number of units inspected}}$$

n = number of units inspected per sample

$$UCL_p = \bar{p} + 3\sqrt{\frac{\bar{p}\ (1 - \bar{p}\ )}{n}} \qquad LCL_p = \bar{p} - 3\sqrt{\frac{\bar{p}\ (1 - \bar{p}\ )}{n}}$$

Use the p chart with either constant or changing sample sizes. When n changes, UCL_p and LCL_p must be recalculated. LCL_p must be equal to or greater than 0; LCL_p can never be less than 0.

np chart

$$n\bar{p} = \frac{\text{Total number of non-conforming units}}{\text{Total number of units inspected}}$$

$n\bar{p}$ = number of units inspected per sample

$$UCL_{np} = n\bar{p} + 3\sqrt{n\bar{p}\ (1 - \bar{p}\ )} \qquad LCL_{np} = n\bar{p} - 3\sqrt{n\bar{p}\ (1 - \bar{p}\ )}$$

Use the np chart with constant sample sizes. When n changes, UCL_{np} and LCL_{np} must be recalculated. LCL_{np} must be equal to or greater than 0; LCL_{np} can never be less than 0.

c chart

$$\bar{c} = \frac{\text{Total number of defects}}{\text{Number of samples}}$$

$$\text{UCL}_c = \bar{c} + 3\sqrt{\bar{c}} \qquad\qquad \text{LCL}_c = \bar{c} - 3\sqrt{\bar{c}}$$

Use the c chart when the number of units inspected per sample is constant. LCL_c must be equal to or greater than 0; LCL_c can never be less than 0.

u chart

$$\bar{u} = \frac{\text{Total number of defects}}{\text{Total number of units inspected}}$$

n = number of units inspected per sample

$$\text{UCL}_u = \bar{u} + 3\sqrt{\bar{u}/n} \qquad\qquad \text{LCL}_u = \bar{u} - 3\sqrt{\bar{u}/n}$$

Use the u chart when the number of units inspected per sample is not constant. When n changes, UCL_u and LCL_u must be recalculated. LCL_u must be equal to or greater than 0; LCL_u can never be less than 0.

X-bar chart for sample averages

$\overline{X}$ = average for each sample

$$UCL_x = \overline{\overline{X}} + A_2 * \overline{R}$$

$$LCL_x = \overline{\overline{X}} - A_2 * \overline{R}$$

$$\overline{\overline{X}} = \frac{\text{Sum of } \overline{X} \text{ values for all subgroups}}{\text{Number of subgroups}}$$

$$UCL_x = \overline{\overline{X}} + A_3 * \overline{s}$$

$$LCL_x = \overline{\overline{X}} - A_3 * \overline{s}$$

R chart for sample ranges

R = range for each subgroup

$$\overline{R} = \frac{\text{Sum of ranges for all subgroups}}{\text{Number of subgroups}}$$

$$UCL_R = D_4 * \overline{R} \qquad\qquad LCL_R = D_3 * \overline{R}$$

S chart for sample sigmas

S = Sigma for each subgroup

$$\bar{s} = \frac{\text{Sum of sigmas for all subgroups}}{\text{Number of subgroups}}$$

$$UCL_s = B_4 * \bar{s} \qquad\qquad LCL_s = B_3 * \bar{s}$$

Capability & performance indices

Cp/Pp

$$Cp/Pp = \frac{\text{Specification width}}{\text{Natural tolerance}}$$

$$Cp = \frac{USL - LSL}{6\sigma_{est}}$$

$$Pp = \frac{USL - LSL}{6\sigma_{calc}}$$

$$\sigma_{est} = \bar{R}/d_2$$

Pc/Pr

$$Pc/Pr = \frac{\text{Natural tolerance}}{\text{Specification width}}$$

$$Pc = \frac{6\sigma_{est}}{USL - LSL}$$

$$Pr = \frac{6\sigma_{calc}}{USL - LSL}$$

$$\sigma_{calc} = \sqrt{\frac{\Sigma(X - \bar{X})^2}{n}}$$

Cpm

$$\sigma_{Cpm} = \sqrt{\frac{\Sigma(X - Nom)}{n - 1}}$$

$$Cpm = \frac{USL - LSL}{6 * \sigma_{Cpm}}$$

Cpk

$$Z_U = \frac{USL - \overline{\overline{X}}}{\sigma_{est}} \qquad Z_L = \frac{\overline{\overline{X}} - LSL}{\sigma_{est}}$$

$Cpk = $ Minimum of $Z_U / 3$ or $Z_L / 3$

Ppk

$$Z_U = \frac{USL - \overline{\overline{X}}}{\sigma_{calc}} \qquad Z_L = \frac{\overline{\overline{X}} - LSL}{\sigma_{calc}}$$

$Ppk = $ Minimum of $Z_U / 3$ or $Z_L / 3$

Median & R chart formulae

$\widetilde{X}$ = median for each sample

$\widetilde{\widetilde{X}}$ = median of $\widetilde{X}$ values for all subgroups

$UCL_x = \widetilde{\widetilde{X}} + A_5 \widetilde{R}$

$LCL_x = \widetilde{\widetilde{X}} - A_5 \widetilde{R}$

R = range for each subgroup

$\widetilde{R}$ = median of ranges for subgroups

$UCL_R = D_4 \widetilde{R}$

$LCL_R = D_3 \widetilde{R}$

3 chart formulae

Subgroup-to-subgroup value of X-bar

$$UCL = \overline{\overline{X}} + E_2\overline{MR}$$

$$LCL \quad \overline{\overline{X}} - E_2\overline{MR}$$

Subgroup-to-subgroup value of MR

$$UCL = D_4\overline{MR}$$

$$LCL = D_3\overline{MR}$$

Within subgroup values of R

$$UCL = D_4\overline{R}$$

$$LCL = D_3\overline{R}$$

Factors for 3 charts

Where k refers to the size of the moving range and n refers to the subgroup size of individuals:

$\overline{\overline{X}}$		MR & R			
k	E_2	n	D_4	D_3	d_2
2	2.66	2	3.267	0	1.128
3	1.77	3	2.575	0	1.693
4	1.46	4	2.284	0	2.059
5	1.29	5	2.114	0	2.326

Gage R&R formulae

Repeatability: Equipment variation (EV)

$$EV = \overline{\overline{R}} * K_1 \qquad \%EV = 100[EV/TV]$$

Reproducibility: Appariser variation (AV)

$$AV = \sqrt{[(\overline{\overline{X}}_{DIFF} * K_2)^2 - (EV_2/nr)]} \qquad \%AV = 100[AV/TV]$$

Repeatability & reproducibility (R&R)

$$R\&R = \sqrt{[(EV^2 + AV^2)]} \qquad \%R\&R = 100[R\&R/TV]$$

Part variation (PV)

$$PV = R_p * K_3 \qquad \%PV = 100[PV/TV]$$

Total variation (TV)

$$TV = \sqrt{(R\&R^2 + PV^2)}$$

Acceptability

$$Acceptability = \frac{Total\ Gage\ Capability\ (R\&R)}{Specification\ Tolerance}$$

K factors for Gage R&R

K Factors for Gage R&R		
Trials	*K₁*	
2	4.56	
3	3.05	
Appraisers	2	3
K₂	3.65	2.70
Parts	*K₃*	
2	3.65	
3	2.70	
4	2.30	
5	2.08	
6	1.93	
7	1.82	
8	1.74	
9	1.67	
10	1.62	

Appendix B

Values for Confidence Intervals

		Confidence Bounds				
df	.99	.95	.90	.10	.05	.01
1	0.00016	0.00393	0.01579	2.70554	3.84147	6.63486
2	0.02010	0.10259	0.21072	4.60517	5.99147	9.21034
3	0.11483	0.35185	0.58438	6.25139	7.81472	11.34489
4	0.29711	0.71072	1.06362	7.77944	9.48773	13.27671
5	0.55429	1.14547	1.61030	9.23635	11.07050	15.08634
6	0.87207	1.63538	2.20413	10.64464	12.59159	16.81190
7	1.23903	2.16734	2.83311	12.01704	14.06716	18.47535
8	1.64646	2.73263	3.48953	13.36157	15.50732	20.09024
9	2.08785	3.32511	4.16816	14.68367	16.91899	21.66602
10	2.55819	3.94029	4.86517	15.98718	18.30704	23.20925
11	3.05349	4.57481	5.57778	17.27502	19.67515	24.72498
12	3.57050	5.22602	6.30378	18.54935	21.02607	26.21697
13	4.10688	5.89185	7.04149	19.81194	22.36204	27.68825
14	4.66038	6.57062	7.78953	21.06414	23.68479	29.14124
15	5.22928	7.26091	8.54675	22.30713	24.99579	30.57792
16	5.81218	7.96163	9.31223	23.54183	26.29623	31.99993
17	6.40768	8.67174	10.08517	24.76904	27.58711	33.40866
18	7.01482	9.39043	10.86493	25.98942	28.86930	34.80531
19	7.63263	10.11700	11.65090	27.20357	30.14353	36.19087
20	8.26031	10.85080	12.44261	28.41198	31.41043	37.56624
21	8.89705	11.59130	13.23960	29.61509	32.67057	38.93217

df	.99	.95	.90		.10	.05	.01
22	9.54237	12.33801	14.04148		30.81328	33.92444	40.28936
23	10.19561	13.09050	14.84796		32.00690	35.17246	41.63840
24	10.85627	13.84839	15.65867		33.19625	36.41503	42.97982
25	11.52394	14.61141	16.47341		34.38159	37.65248	44.31411
26	12.19805	15.37915	17.29188		35.56317	38.88514	45.64168
27	12.87839	16.15139	18.11390		36.74122	40.11327	46.96294
28	13.56457	16.92785	18.93923		37.91592	41.33714	48.27824
29	14.25633	17.70837	19.76773		39.08747	42.55697	49.58789
30	14.95331	18.49266	20.59921		40.25602	43.77297	50.89218
40	22.16411	26.50928	29.05051		51.80506	55.75848	63.69074
50	29.70653	34.76421	37.68862		63.16712	67.50481	76.15389
60	37.48483	43.18794	46.45889		74.39701	79.08195	88.37942
70	45.44150	51.73926	55.32892		85.52705	90.53123	100.42519
80	53.53993	60.39142	64.27780		96.57820	101.87947	112.32880
90	61.75399	69.12598	73.29109		107.56501	113.14527	124.11632
100	70.06472	77.92946	82.35813		118.49801	124.34212	135.80672

Appendix C

Table of Constants for Control Charts

Sub-group Size	$\overline{X}$ & R Charts				$\overline{X}$ & s Charts			
	Chart for Averages ($\overline{X}$)	Chart for Ranges (R)			Chart for Averages ($\overline{X}$)	Chart for Ranges (R)		
	Factors for Control Limits	Divisors for Estimate of Standard Deviation	Factors for Control Limits		Factors for Control Limits	Divisors for Estimate of Standard Deviation	Factors for Control Limits	
n	A_2	d_2	D_3	D_4	A_3	c_4	B_3	B_4
2	1.880	1.128	—	3.267	2.659	0.7979	—	3.267
3	1.023	1.693	—	2.574	1.954	0.8862	—	2.568
4	0.729	2.059	—	2.282	1.628	0.9213	—	2.266
5	0.577	2.326	—	2.114	1.427	0.9400	—	2.089
6	0.483	2.534	—	2.004	1.287	0.9515	0.030	1.970
7	0.419	2.704	0.076	1.924	1.182	0.9594	0.118	1.882
8	0.373	2.847	0.136	1.864	1.099	0.9650	0.185	1.815
9	0.337	2.970	0.184	1.816	1.032	0.9693	0.239	1.761
10	0.308	3.078	0.223	1.777	0.975	0.9727	0.284	1.716
11	0.285	3.173	0.256	1.744	0.927	0.9754	0.321	1.679
12	0.266	3.258	0.283	1.717	0.886	0.9776	0.354	1.646
13	0.249	3.336	0.307	1.693	0.850	0.9794	0.382	1.618

Sub-group Size	$\overline{X}$ & R Charts				$\overline{X}$ & s Charts			
	Chart for Averages ($\overline{X}$)	Chart for Ranges (R)			Chart for Averages ($\overline{X}$)	Chart for Ranges (R)		
	Factors for Control Limits	Divisors for Estimate of Standard Deviation	Factors for Control Limits		Factors for Control Limits	Divisors for Estimate of Standard Deviation	Factors for Control Limits	
n	A_2	d_2	D_3	D_4	A_3	c_4	B_3	B_4
14	0.235	3.407	0.328	1.672	0.817	0.9810	0.406	1.594
15	0.223	3.472	0.347	1.653	0.789	0.9823	0.428	1.572
16	0.212	3.532	0.363	1.637	0.763	0.9835	0.448	1.552
17	0.203	3.588	0.378	1.622	0.739	0.9845	0.466	1.534
18	0.194	3.640	0.391	1.608	0.718	0.9854	0.482	1.518
19	0.187	3.689	0.403	1.597	0.698	0.9862	0.497	1.503
20	0.180	3.735	0.415	1.585	0.680	0.9869	0.510	1.490
21	0.173	3.778.	0.425	1.575	0.663	0.9876	0.523	1.477
22	0.167	3.819	0.434	1.566	0.647	0.9882	0.534	1.466
23	0.162	3.858	0.443	1.557	0.633	0.9887	0.545	1.455
24	0.157	3.895	0.451	1.548	0.619	0.9892	0.555	1.445
25	0.153	3.931	0.459	1.541	0.606	.9896	0.565	1.435

	Median Charts				Individuals Charts			
	Chart for Medians ($\widetilde{X}$)	Chart for Ranges (R)			Chart for Individuals (X)	Chart for Ranges (R)		
Sub-group Size	Factors for Control Limits	Divisors for Estimate of Standard Deviation	Factors for Control Limits		Factors for Control Limits	Divisors for Estimate of Standard Deviation	Factors for Control Limits	
n	A_2	d_2	D_3	D_4	A_2	d_2	D_3	D_4
2	1.880	1.28	—	3.267	2.660	1.128	—	3.267
3	1.187	1.693	—	2.574	1.772	1.693	—	2.574
4	0.796	2.059	—	2.282	1.457	2.059	—	2.282
5	0.691	2.326	—	2.114	1.290	2.326	—	2.114
6	0.548	2.534	—	2.004	1.184	2.534	—	2.004
7	0.508	2.704	0.076	1.924	1.109	2.704	0.076	1.924
8	0.433	2.847	0.136	1.864	1.054	2.847	0.136	1.864
9	0.412	2.970	0.184	1.816	1.010	2.970	0.184	1.816
10	0.362	3.078	0.223	1.777	0.975	3.078	0.223	1.777

Appendix D

Z scores (% out of spec)

Z	.09	.08	.07	.06	.05	.04	.03	.02	.01	.00	Z
-4.0										.00003	**4.0**
-3.9	.00003	.00003	.00004	.00004	.00004	.00004	.00004	.00004	.00005	.00005	**3.9**
-3.8	.00005	.00005	.00005	.00006	.00006	.00006	.00006	.00007	.00007	.00007	**3.8**
-3.7	.00008	.00008	.00008	.00008	.00009	.00009	.00010	.00010	.00010	.00011	**3.7**
-3.6	.00016	.00015	.00015	.00014	.00014	.00013	.00013	.00012	.00012	.00011	**3.6**
-3.5	.00017	.00017	.00018	.00019	.00019	.00020	.00021	.00022	.00022	.00023	**3.5**
-3.4	.00024	.00025	.00026	.00027	.00028	.00029	.00030	.00031	.00032	.00034	**3.4**
-3.3	.00035	.00036	.00038	.00039	.00040	.00042	.00043	.00045	.00047	.00048	**3.3**
-3.2	.00050	.00052	.00054	.00056	.00058	.00060	.00062	.00064	.00066	.00069	**3.2**
-3.1	.00071	.00074	.00076	.00079	.00082	.00084	.00087	.00090	.00094	.00097	**3.1**
-3.0	.00100	.00104	.00107	.00111	.00114	.00118	.00122	.00126	.00131	.00135	**3.0**
-2.9	.0114	.0014	.0015	.0015	.0016	.0016	.0017	.0018	.0018	.0019	**2.9**
-2.8	.0019	.0020	.0021	..0021	.0022	.0023	.0023	.0024	.0025	.0026	**2.8**
-2.7	.0026	.0027	.0028	.0029	.0030	.0031	.0032	.0033	.0034	.0035	**2.7**
-2.6	.0036	.0037	.0038	.0039	.0040	.0041	.0043	.0044	.0045	.0047	**2.6**
-2.5	.0048	.0049	.0051	.0052	.0054	.0055	.0057	.0059	.0060	.0062	**2.5**
-2.4	.0064	.0066	.0068	.0069	.0071	.0073	.0075	.0078	.0080	.0082	**2.4**
-2.3	.0084	.0087	.0089	.0091	.0094	.0096	.0099	.0102	.0104	.0107	**2.3**
-2.2	.0110	.0113	.0116	.0119	.0122	.0125	.0129	.0132	.0136	.0139	**2.2**
-2.1	.0143	.0146	.0150	.0154	.0158	.0162	.0166	.0170	.0174	.0179	**2.1**

Z	.09	.08	.07	.06	.05	.04	.03	.02	.01	.00	Z
-2.0	.0183	.0188	.0192	.0197	.0202	.0207	.0212	.0217	.0222	.0228	2.0
-1.9	.0233	.0239	.0244	.0250	.0256	.0262	.0268	.0274	.0281	.0287	1.9
-1.8	.0294	.0301	.0307	.0314	.0322	.0329	.0336	.0344	.0351	.0359	1.8
-1.7	.0367	.0375	.0384	.0392	.0401	.0409	.0418	.0427	.0436	.0446	1.7
-1.6	.0455	.0465	.0475	.0485	.0495	.0505	.0516	.0526	.0537	.0548	1.6
-1.5	.0559	.0571	.0582	.0594	.0606	.0618	0630	.0643	.0655	.0668	1.5
-1.4	.0681	.0694	.0708	.0721	.0735	.0749	.0764	.0778	.0793	.0808	1.4
-1.3	.0823	.0838	.0853	.0869	.0885	.0901	.0918	.0934	.0951	.0968	1.3
-1.2	.0985	.1003	.1020	.1038	.1056	.1075	.1093	.1112	.1131	.1151	1.2
-1.1	.1170	.1190	.1210	.1230	.1251	.1271	.1292	.1314	.1335	.1357	1.1
-1.0	.1379	.1401	.1423	.1446	.1469	.1492	.1515	.1539	.1562	.1587	1.0
-0.9	.1611	.1635	.1660	.1685	.1711	.1736	.1762	.1788	.1814	.1841	0.9
-0.8	.1867	.1849	.1922	.1949	.1977	.2005	.2033	.2061	.2090	.2119	0.8
-0.7	.2148	.2117	.2206	.2236	.2266	.2297	.2327	.2358	.2389	.2420	0.7
-0.6	.2451	.2483	.2514	.2546	.2578	.2611	.2643	.2676	.2709	.2743	0.6
-0.5	.2776	.2810	.2843	.2877	.2912	.2946	.2981	.3015	.3050	.3085	0.5
-0.4	.3121	.3156	.3192	.3228	.3264	.3300	.3336	.3372	.3409	.3446	0.4
-0.3	.3483	.3520	.3557	.3594	.3632	.3669	.3707	.3745	.3783	.3821	0.3
-0.2	.3859	.3897	.3936	.3974	.4013	.4052	.4090	.4129	.4168	.4207	0.2
-0.1	.4247	.4286	.4325	.4364	.4404	.4443	.4483	.4522	.4562	.4602	0.1
-0.0	.4641	.4681	.4721	.4761	.4801	.4840	.4880	.4920	.4960	.5000	0.0

Index